In the
Same
Boat

Enjoy the
Laugh Breaks!
"Mary Pat"
Welshans

In the Same Boat

55 Laugh Breaks for Frazzled Moms

By Humor Columnist and Fellow Frazzled Mom
Mary Beth Weisenburger

Second Edition

FreeBird

PUBLISHING AND PROMOTIONS

In the Same Boat
By Mary Beth Weisenburger

Published by
FreeBird Publishing and Promotions
22273 Road D
Continental OH 45831

www.marybethw.com
www.freebirdpromotions.com

Printed in the United States of America

ISBN 978-0-615-27453-9

"A cheerful heart is good medicine"
-Proverbs 17:22

DEDICATION

To all you frazzled moms out there--smile, laugh
and remember that the rest of us have
only one oar in the water, too!

CONTENTS

CONTENTS (Continued)

THE HOLIDAYS: GOING OVERBOARD

LIFE IN GENERAL: MAKING WAVES

A SPECIAL TRIBUTE

NOTE TO THE READER

Dear Reader,

Thank you for your interest in this book. By merely picking it up, you have confirmed a number of things:

1.) You have children; and therefore--

2.) You try desperately to maintain a sense of humor; and therefore--

3.) You are in the same boat with multitudes of other frazzled moms who need a constant infusion of laugh therapy to make it through the rough waters of motherhood, marriage and life in general!

While the columns you are about to read started out as my attempt at documenting the funny side of my family life, I quickly learned from my readers' feedback that these stories strike a universal funny bone. We can all relate to crazy, comical home life situations that even Ripley's would at times find hard to believe. But in the ordinary busy-ness of our lives we need to remind ourselves to stop and appreciate these gifts of humor that come our way on a daily (and sometimes hourly) basis.

I invite you to come on board! Enjoy the "sounds familiar" observations found in *Motherhood: Rough Seas Ahead*, the seasonal extremes in *The Holidays: Going Overboard* and the run-ins with life's little absurdities in *Life in General: Making Waves*. The stories are guaranteed to make you and frazzled moms everywhere smile and realize--we're all *In the Same Boat!*

Sincerely,

Mary Beth Weisenburger

A Fellow Frazzled Mom

ACKNOWLEDGEMENTS

To my husband Steve, who has laughed along with
me for a quarter of a century--I love you.

To my children, Curtis and Erin--thanks for the
endless inspiration. You are gifts from God and I love
you both. And remember--as long as I'm living,
my babies you'll be.

To my mom and dad--thanks for bestowing me with
the coping skill of humor in everyday life.

To my wonderful, witty friend and colleague Rachel--
thank you for the coaching and cajoling. You and the
Banker Babes are true friends. Sunshine Always!

To the fellow writers of the Black Swamp Writer's
Group--Dave, Karen, Nancy and the whole gang--
thanks for the early infusion of support,
encouragement, and caffeine.

MOTHERHOOD:
Rough Seas Ahead

OUT OF THE MOUTHS OF BABES

There was a time not very long ago when I lived to hear the sounds of my children's voices. From their very first coos, I was hooked on their magical, musical utterances, and I did everything I could to speed up their language development. I read to my children even before they were born, so they would have expanded vocabularies. I impatiently coaxed them to say the crown jewel of all words--"momma"--and I flatly denied that they both said "dada" first. I meticulously recorded each new word in their baby books and felt oh-so-smug about their early progress.

I was especially relieved when my children could finally verbalize "where it hurts," so I would no longer have to guess what was wrong. Then came the night I was rocking my feverish three-year-old, working on getting his temperature down to a point where my mind would stop forming images of oxygen tents and Pediatric Intensive Care Units. As he fidgeted in my lap and rested his weak little hand on my bare shin, he said in a feeble voice, "Mommy, would you do me a favor?" "Sure, honey," I answered. "What is it? Do you want another cool cloth on your forehead?" I swear to you, his reply was this: "Will you please shave your legs?"

I had created a monster. Actually, two of them. I started to feel a bit like Doctor Frankenstein, whose experiment went so awry.

Soon, my son was informing the grocery store check-out lady that his mommy was wearing pajamas under her long coat. When he was tested for preschool, he was asked to describe the drawing he made of his family. It went like this: "That's my mom. I gave her brown hair because that's the REAL color it is. And that's my dad. See all those big lines on his forehead?"

Nothing was sacred. My precocious little girl would answer the phone and tell the caller that daddy was "in the bathroom reading." She would ask people why their noses were so big or why they were SMOKING. And once, at age two, she stood on a chair in a restaurant and recited this little ditty at the top of her voice, to the great amusement of the entire wait staff: "Ladies and gentleman, take my advice: pull down your pants and slide on the ice!"

My little storytellers are older now, but that does not mean I'm off the hook. Just last week my chatty 11-year-old proclaimed, in the midst of a group of neighbors, that I really had MANY MORE gray hairs on my head than she thought.

I wonder where *those* came from?

MORNING OLYMPICS

Every four years, I tune in to the Olympics and watch lean, lithe bodies clad in red, white and blue spandex do amazing things. They perform twists in mid-air, sled head first at breakneck speeds, and dance on ice like they have never heard of gravity. Well, as awesome as those athletes are, I have news for them:

They are no match for mothers on school mornings.

I call it the Morning Olympics. To get a gold medal you must get your kids up, washed, dressed, fed and out the door with all necessities and in suitable outerwear before the bus driver honks the horn for the third time and without proclaiming "Hurry Up! You're going to be late!" more than 125 times. It's a battle against the clock that no Olympic participant would want to take on, top in their sport or not.

I myself seem to be stuck in the less-desirable silver medalist category lately. Though I have trained for this event for years, I can't seem to master it. Let's have a look at my team's recent highlight films:

The Starting Gun

This is when the various alarms go off in our house, attempting to rouse all Morning Olympics contestants. One alarm blasts country music at an excruciating decibel level while another shouts the news. A third one plinks out the tune of "Old MacDonald Had A Farm" over and over, not realizing that the team member who owns this alarm is still in some sort of heavy REM sleep which prevents any sound from piercing his brain for at least 20 more minutes. The fourth alarm ekes out only a few tones before its groggy owner (the team's male Captain) repeatedly raps it over the head in search of a sleep button. Points are taken off for these "delay of game" tactics.

The Missing Clothes Competition
Once we're off and running, it's time to find a very cool and coordinated outfit for team member #1. This outfit choice is terribly important, as it must stand up to the scrutiny of 18 other third graders who will most certainly note if today's shirt is almost the same color as yesterday's shirt. Penalty time is added if the desired clothing item is in the laundry room downstairs or in a wad under the bed. The second contestant in the Morning Olympics has made it very clear from the time he was two that picking out and/or changing clothes ranks right up there with a visit to the dentist on his "least favorite things to do" list. Consequently, he despises this portion of the games, and consistently tries to bypass it by doing such things as sleeping in his school clothes the night before, or dressing with only one eye open so he can stay "half asleep." These infractions are against the rules, not to mention incredibly annoying to the female Captain of this team.

The What's For Breakfast Bout
This is the point where things get really hairy, so the male Captain of the team decides his work here is done and, after a merry round of kisses and good-byes, departs with a smile on his face and his sanity intact. This leaves the other Captain (me) not only outnumbered but also wondering if trades are possible in this sport.

The venue is the same every morning:
Remaining Captain: What would you like for breakfast?
Team members: What is there?
Captain: Well, there's Frosted Fruities, Jumbo Cornies and Wheatie O's. Just like yesterday. And the day before that.
Team member #1: Oh. (Pause) I'd like Cinnamon Krunchies, please.
Team member #2: I'm not hungry. Can I have a Pepsi?

This unsportsmanlike conduct calls for swift course correction from the Captain.

For the sake of column space, I will not even go into the ensuing Take Your Vitamin Challenge.

The Lunch Money Relay
After breakfast and the obligatory battles over the sinks while brushing teeth, it's time to wrap up loose ends and gather speed for the final leg of the Olympic race. It's the Lunch Money Relay event. This means we must locate the dollar bills left over from yesterday's lunch (right front pocket of the jeans lying on the closet floor upstairs), and transfer them to the appropriate place for today's lunch (red zippered wallet in the blue book bag). This is easier said than done, as it is a well known fact that all children's closets in my house are mini-versions of the Bermuda Triangle, meaning important things such as lunch money will mysteriously disappear even though it was there just a minute ago. Really.

Then, just when we are ready to head out the door, one team member casually mentions that he has already racked up several charges in the lunch room and that he won't even be allowed to ENTER the cafeteria today unless he brings in 12 dollars and 35 cents. This announcement causes a major stir along with a massive deduction of points, and the team learns that bonus points are not awarded if the Captain has to slowly count to 10 while frantically scrounging for additional cash.

The School Bus Dash
Finally, the team readies for the last event. Over the course of the one minute and 22 seconds remaining, all members must find a coat, hat and gloves, don the correct book bag, scramble around the garage to feed and water dogs, cats and bunnies, and take any and all garbage and mail with them to the end of the driveway without dropping anything along the way.

Whew. Is it any wonder a gold medal is out of my reach?

Sadly, the Morning Olympics, while common in many American households, go mostly unrecognized. For this reason I must take the opportunity to publicly say congratulations to all you moms out there who regularly compete in these Olympics and win. You truly deserve a gold medal. Go ahead--grab a bouquet of flowers, stand on a kitchen chair and hum a few bars of the national anthem.

But don't bask in the glory too long because in a few short hours, the Homework Hurdles begin.

THE PLAY HOUSE

Many of you out there may be thinking about remodeling your home or even building a new one. "This sounds like fun!" you say cheerfully. You know it will take much planning, drawing, organization and piles of cash to complete your dream project. You will spend hours, days and months making sure things go well. But you will probably forget something, as I did. You will forget to gather input from your children on how your design will REALLY be interpreted once it's finished. This is a bad thing to forget.

If you have children, your house will become a Children's Play House. Period. Allow me to elaborate.

Say you wanted a nice big living room with high ceilings so you would have a wonderful feeling of openness. That was your full intention. In reality, this is what you have done: you have created an indoor gymnasium. Those tall ceilings are perfect for kids to practice catching pop flies, the openness you love practically *begs* for a game of Frisbee, and the floor space is now transformed into a gymnastics arena for your eight-year-old, so you are not allowed to put the new coffee table where it belongs. Silly you!

Of course, I am speaking from personal experience here. In addition to my misguided idea of what a living room should be, I messed up in other areas. Let's take the stairway for instance. My intent: "What a beautiful staircase and loft, where I will someday watch my only daughter descend gracefully in her prom dress." The kids' interpretation: "Hey! Mom and Dad just gave us the coolest slide! And check out the loft--let's get some fishing poles and see if we can catch the cat when it walks below us!"

In my ignorance, I also missed the following "Children's Play House" realities:

1. Any extended hallway will soon have basketball rims posted on both ends to facilitate all-out, full-court play.
2. A new home office and computer will be completely overtaken by pre-teens who, let's face it, know way more about computers than we adults do.
3. If a kitchen bar is installed, children of the house will be lulled into thinking they live in a fast-food restaurant, where they can demand to eat at all hours and never have to clean up.
4. Children's bedrooms are an unnecessary, simply decorative space. Kids are either sleeping over at someone else's house, "accidentally" falling asleep on the living room couch or trying to con their way into their parents' bed.
5. Go ahead and remove the refrigerator door. You know it will not stay closed anyway.
6. New furniture, no matter how lovely, will be tipped over to make a fort, and cushions will be fashioned into battle shields.

I hope this list helps any parent about to build or remodel. If I would have known these things, I could have saved a lot of time and money.

Not to mention a few cats.

BEDTIME STALLING 101

I have heard some very shocking news lately. A friend of mine told me she knows a woman whose cousin's kid in California somewhere actually walks into her living room every night at precisely 8:30 p.m. and announces to those present that she is now going to bed. And then, weirdly, SHE GOES TO BED! What kind of household must this be?? I suppose there could be some children in this world who go to bed with little or no fuss, but I don't know of any personally. In fact, my children have obviously taken some sort of extensive training and have already earned honorary degrees in the fine art of Bedtime Stalling.

I imagine the curriculum a kid must complete in order to receive this diploma includes such critical components as How to Disappear at the Right Moment, Creatively Extending Deadlines, and Fast Talking and Excuse Making at Bedtime. These topics are covered in the following courses that I know my precious offspring have passed with flying colors:

Strategic Delay Tactics 101

This is the basic course and can be taken by kids as young as two. Students learn how to feign hearing loss when called to go to bed, demand marathon story-telling sessions, and concoct complaints of ill-fitting PJ's and maybe even a tummy ache, for good measure. As they get older, they add protestations such as "Only a few more minutes--the show's almost over," and "None of my friends have to go to bed this early." Then there is the Alternative Suggestion Tact--"Can I sleep (fill in the blank) instead?" Options presented could range from "in your bed" to "on the couch" to "with the cats in the garage." Then there's the

"Houdini." You THINK they have gone to bed but when you decide to trek upstairs to check on them, they're NOT THERE AT ALL. And never have been.

Security Testing 201

This course covers the all-important safety and security checks that must be conducted prior to anyone even considering closing his or her eyelids. We do not bother with the obvious tasks such as locking doors and windows. No, those things are reserved for rational adults. In this class, success is reached when all real and imaginary monsters have been chased from under beds and behind dressers, and satisfactory answers have been given to the inevitable "What's That Noise??" question. Once I spent an entire hour convincing my little "students" that the scratching on the window was truly a branch from a nearby tree, and not a long bony finger of a potential intruder. Our big Yellow Lab Zoey is often summoned upstairs to perform an investigative once-over and make sure nothing is amiss.

Environmental Controls & Fluid Adjustment 301

Is it too hot? The overhead fan needs to be on. Blankets too scratchy? Eliminate one. Too cold now? Fan goes off and new blanket (softer and fuzzier version) goes on. Then we must proceed to the tucking-in ceremony. One child requires a mummy-like swaddling and two pillows wedged under his head. The other likes the free wheeling approach where her feet can "breathe" out the sides of the blanket. In addition, she must be accompanied by the stuffed animal currently in favor and a Sponge Bob blanket. The amount of light exposure is then analyzed. Is the hallway light on? Closet light off? Door open just a crack?

This course emphasizes that fluid adjustments are only effective when made at the very last minute--perhaps a glass of ice water is necessary for proper sleep conditions. (Ice water from the kitchen downstairs that is, not a plain glass of water from the upstairs bathroom.) And speaking of bathroom, yes, we need to make one last trip, which then requires a re-tucking-in ceremony.

Memory Loss 500
This is my personal favorite, and it's the crown jewel equivalent of a doctorate degree in Bedtime Stalling. Just when you relax and let your guard down, thinking all is well for the night, a small voice calls out the words that cause a heart to stop: "Mom? I forgot..."
This is followed by
   a.) "...I told the teacher you would bring treats for the whole class tomorrow."
   b.) "...my science project is due. Do we have 12 different kinds of leaves and the scientific names for each of them?"
   c.) "...I left my tadpole collection in my jeans pockets. Did you wash them yet?" or
   d.) "...I really need to ask you something--is it OK that I invited my class over for my birthday?"
When my children were babies, I longed for the time when they would sleep through the night and bedtimes would become routine. I was definitely unaware that Bedtime Stalling was an accomplished art form and would continue to be developed and refined until they moved out to get a real college degree someday. Then I suppose I'll be the one who won't be able to sleep...

CLEANING OUT THE VAN

At my house, cleaning out the family van is a "sentinel event." This means two things: 1.) It happens only rarely; and 2.) When it does, it is not a positive experience.

I admit it, the van/taxi I drive as a busy mom is far from orderly. When we do get around to cleaning it out, the scene resembles the aftermath of a tornado-- when people pick through the rubble and discover miscellaneous items strewn about in strange and unusual ways. It's an ugly chore and no one wants to do it. The only high point comes when one of the reluctant car cleaners finds something slightly valuable. "So THAT'S where that went!" says the proud excavator.

This is not an exaggeration. If you were to peer into my van today, for example, you would find standard fare such as candy wrappers, church bulletins, coloring books coupled with half-melted crayons, a way-past-prime french fry or two, spent tissues, ball gloves, golf clubs, a phone book, umbrellas, ice scrapers, CD's, videotapes, empty juice boxes, errant homework papers and a host of McDonald's toys that most certainly multiply when no one is looking. And that doesn't include the various articles of clothing that are doing time in my van: socks, two coats, an $11.00 floppy hat my daughter HAD to have and promised would NEVER leave her head, tiny doll shoes, one big kid shoe and a pair of winter gloves. At times, I could outfit the entire Brady Bunch with the cast-off clothing in my van. Then there are the not-so-standard items. Yesterday I had to move a hard hat and safety glasses out of the way before my passenger could sit down.

And once, we located a lost and extremely mummified toad in the side pocket of the sliding door, a victim of my son's plan to "scare mommy in the morning" by putting a live toad in my cup holder. We honestly searched for two weeks for the little critter, always with the sliding door open of course.

This kind of chaos could come in handy some day, I rationalize. If they ever bring back the game show "Let's Make A Deal," where they ask contestants to produce off-the-wall items from their purses or bags, I can pull up in my van and tell the rest of the audience to go home. Monty Hall would be proud.

My husband is a different story.

He often reminds me of the days before children when our sporty little cars would be gleaming on the outside and spotless on the inside. He shakes his head in disbelief at our current situation. This is not progress, in his mind. "It's your fault," I tell him. "You're the one who taught the kids to NEVER throw any trash out the car windows." He is wise and never uses the van unless it's absolutely necessary and he has given seven days notice.

We have made some weak attempts at order. "OK, everybody," I bark. "No one leaves this van without taking three things out with them." It's like shoveling snow while it's still snowing. I do have my sunglasses in one designated spot, the registration safely tucked away in the glove box and an ash tray full of emergency change. But most often, I am heard meekly apologizing to all who enter my "lived-in" vehicle. And I have been known to mumble something to the bag boy at the grocery store about my secret government job that absolutely requires all of this debris as the reason why he can't find room in the back to load my groceries.

I know others who are in similar situations. We are not generally sloppy or lazy people, really. We are simply busy people who are trying to stay on top of too many things. Having a clean vehicle slides to the bottom of the priority list.

Oh, well. The day will come soon enough when my van is once again clean and stays clean because my little passengers are all grown up and polluting their own cars. In the meantime, if the highway patrol ever decides to do random inspections of the INSIDE of vehicles, I'll be picking up trash along the side of the road for countless community service hours for sure.

Hmmm....maybe I *will* clean the van. I don't look very good in stripes.

SHOVELING SNOW WHILE IT'S STILL SNOWING

Here's a favorite quote of mine from Phyllis Diller:

"Cleaning your house while your children are growing is like shoveling snow while it is still snowing."

Lately, I seem to be shoveling a lot. I can do 10 loads of laundry a day, and still never find the bottom of the laundry basket. I can dutifully scrub a kitchen counter only to find it 30 seconds later covered in glitter glue, pipe cleaners and poster paint. And I own a home where toys refuse to be locked away in oppressive containers such as a toy box. Our particular toys like to exercise their constitutional right to live freely in all areas of the house.

Our latest incident? SOMEONE left a green ink pen on the floor and SOMEONE'S DOG found it and decided to chew on it while resting comfortably on my Winter Wheat colored carpeting. SOMEONE then tried to clean it and ended up turning the long, thin, green streak into a long, thick, green, fuzzy stripe. Can a professional carpet cleaner get it out? No. My husband jokes that we now have a foul shot line in our living room, to go with the Ohio State backboard and rim that hangs on the door. I am not amused.

It wasn't always this way. When I think back to the early days of our marriage, in a tiny two-bedroom apartment in the city, I recall our biggest housekeeping hassle was the fact that we sometimes had two days' worth of newspapers on the coffee table or a dirty glass in the sink. Later, we moved into a sparkling new house that was actually easy to keep clean. Then the babies came, and things haven't been the same since.

I know I'm not alone. I have a friend who recently became a father. He can't believe his precious little son has wreaked such havoc on his furniture and flooring. His advice to new parents: Don't fight it--just buy juice colored carpeting and be done with it.

We do have hope. In fact, actual scientists are this very moment using our tax dollars to create a House of the Future to help us. I know this because while visiting a certain well-known multi-cajillion dollar theme park in central Florida recently, my family and I, in the throes of full heat exhaustion, wandered into a nearby air-conditioned pavilion. The pavilion turned out to be an interesting place where the "The House of the Future" was on display. We began our tour with great anticipation, but in the end, I just shook my head in disappointment. The futurist engineers were wasting their time on such things as a Spa Shower with a TV, a mirror that tells you the time and temperature, a fridge with a built-in stove and a front door lock that uses a thumbprint identification system.

I hate to inform them, but that's not the House of the Future I want. Where's the built-in dust busting lasers? Why no junk mail eliminator or automatic school paper sorter? What about the sock matcher and the shoe finder? I need a magic washing machine that continuously washes, dries and folds clothes before zapping them back into the appropriate closets. How about a self-cleaning carpet? Simply push a button and any debris on the carpet gets sucked under the floor and whisked away, preferably to a grouchy neighbor's yard. And those scientists can keep the time and temperature mirror. Give me one that reflects a clean house even when it's dirty or can be programmed to squawk at my kids every time they forget to put something away.

This too shall pass, I know. In the meantime, I'll just have to keep in mind another favorite saying. The author is unknown, but I'll bet money a mom wrote it:

"Cleaning and scrubbing can wait for tomorrow
For babies grow up, we've learned to our sorrow.
So quiet down cobwebs, dust go to sleep.
I'm rocking my baby, and babies don't keep."

A BETTER BABY SHOWER

I was waiting with my overflowing grocery cart in an endless checkout line last week when my gaze fell on a picture of cute babies frolicking on the cover of a book. "How to host the BEST BABY SHOWER EVER!" the title proclaimed.

Huh! I scoffed. I had a great baby shower, complete with baby wipe warmers, the latest model of stroller with luggage rack and VCR, and the entire collection of Winnie the Pooh, classic version. But, 12 years of motherhood later, reality has set in.

I really could have used a better shower.

A shower that would have taken me past the naïve babyhood years into full-fledged childhood, when I really needed an arsenal of specialty items. A survival kit, of sorts. No Doctor Spock books here, no. Too theoretical. What I needed was a treasure chest of practical emergency items to get me through the critical times. It would contain such staples as:

• Pre-constructed school projects, including my personal favorite, the SHOE BOX DIORAMA. Sadistic teachers always ask for these, and children always forget they are due until after you have tucked them in bed for the fourth time. Preference should be given to three-dimensional scenes depicting Native American encampments, as they seem to be required of every second grader. Another helpful gift would be a model of the atom, using "items found in any home," such as popsicle sticks, Velcro and marbles in matching colors. And let's not forget the ever-popular model of the solar system, powered by a revolving mechanism. If you gave this gift at a baby shower, the mother-to-be would probably throw the planet Mars back at you in a hormone-induced frenzy. But believe me, 10 years later she would be in your debt big time.

- A collection of children's birthday party gifts, already wrapped. When I've had less than 24 hours' notice, my kids have been known to show up at parties armed with a half-eaten bag of Skittles and a free pair of panty hose I received in the mail that day. I'm not sure, but I'm guessing some cool gel pens or baseballs would have been more popular.

- Halloween costumes. Enough said.

- Two dozen frosted cupcakes, freezable. These are for the times when your precious offspring announce, three full minutes before the school bus arrives, that oh yeah, they signed your name on the snack list for "some party we are having at school today. What do we have?"

- A miscellaneous box filled with items known to disappear without a trace: permission slips for field trips, a pair of matched socks, sharpened pencils, scissors that actually cut something. And while you're at it, add felt, sequins, markers, pipe cleaners, glue, construction paper, a roll of duct tape, 25 empty toilet paper tubes and all materials needed to produce a group of hand puppets that perfectly resemble the Founding Fathers.

- Bottles and jars with air holes already punched in the lids for the variety of homeless animals, reptiles and insects that will come to live with you unexpectedly. Take care not to make the holes in the lids too large, as you may be surprised just how tiny hundreds of newly-hatched praying mantises are. I know I was.

This concept could truly be the start of something revolutionary--a whole new tradition! I'm thinking it has spin-off possibilities as well. Why, just the other day, I was throwing out the last bath towel I had received as a wedding shower gift.

Hmmm…a second wedding shower?

CLOSET CONFESSIONS

Wanted: One orderly person to wade through and reorganize kids' closets. Must be physically able to move mountains of wadded clothes. Proficient in hanger detangling, sock matching and junk sorting. Experience with rapid growth spurts preferred. Must have all shots.

It's that time of year again: the seasons have changed, and my kids, who received brand new jeans before the start of school, are standing in front of me and demonstrating how they can no longer fasten the top button on the very same jeans. And I can see their ankles are showing. They need new clothes--again. What's even worse is that this situation leads directly to the dreaded semi-annual Kids Closet Excavation, a project of immense proportion that often calls for search parties, front end loaders, metal detectors and the entire closet shelving aisle at the local hardware store.

I try to buy time. "High water pants are IN this year," I tell them. "Don't you want to be IN?" And, "Your dad uses the old Unbutton the Top Button Trick so he doesn't need to buy new pants--try that for awhile." And even, "Your mother has mold allergies and should not be spending any extended periods of time in toxic areas such as your closet."

But slowly and painfully, I realize I can't put it off any longer. The kids are dressing from clothes right out of the dryer and starting to wear their dad's socks. This time, I resolve, things will be different. I will tame those closets, get rid of the too-small clothes and efficiently organize everything on shelves and hangers. I will not try to foist my son's expensive and hardly worn gym shorts on his younger sister by saying "black is a unisex color for gym shorts!" I will not live in a fantasy world and keep the high-water jeans for cut-off shorts next summer, and I will not look at a single one of my daughter's outfits and say it's too cute to part with just yet.

Luckily, I can always turn to the professionals for support. There are scores of books on organizing a household, and it seems every women's magazine routinely offers how-to's on the subject. I may even buy something from those gadget catalogs I receive in the mail every other day--like the *Rolling Pants Trolley Which Conveniently Stores up to 18 Pairs of Pants!* Or the *Super Size Shoe Rack which Puts an End to Frantic Searching On the Closet Floor!* Or, if I am really feeling ambitious, I could purchase the revolutionary Space Saving Bags, fill them up, and use my vacuum to "*Suction Out The Air and Save Valuable Storage Space!*"

More likely, I will buy all new color-coded hangers, throw out the ratty tennies, donate the good stuff to charity and vacuum the floor. I will neatly fold and stack shirts according to the length of sleeve, separate school clothes from play clothes, and buy new jeans that fit, at least for the next month.

And then I will take a picture so next week I can remind myself what the closets looked like the day they were organized.

EIGHTEEN YEARS OF SLEEPLESS NIGHTS

A few years ago, my "little" sister (age 35) became a mom for the first time. Benjamin William came into the world a helpless eight-pound wonder, ready to keep his unsuspecting parents awake for at least the next 18 years.

Now, my sister laughs nervously when I say this to her, but she will learn soon enough, as I did: the middle of the night infant feedings and fussiness eventually go away, but there will be many years afterward of sleepless nights, for a wide variety of reasons. This is not something you find written in the baby books. "Sleeping through the night" is a myth of huge proportions, I tell her. The phrase should be struck from parenting vocabulary.

I illustrate for my still-skeptical sister how a recent week went for me, a mother of an 11-year-old and a 13-year-old, who once enjoyed at least six straight hours of sleep a night:

On Friday night, my daughter asked for the zillionth time if she could have a few friends stay overnight. I was well aware that this was a certain kiss of death if I wanted to have a good night's sleep, but she had been chip, chip, chipping away at me for days until I had a weak moment. So, two cute little girls complete with 12 overnight bags came to our house and proceeded to not slumber. Husband and I settled in around 11:00 p.m. At around 12:30 a.m., I used my "stern mom voice" to tell the gaggle of giggling girls it was time to go to sleep. At 1:30 a.m., I elbowed my snoring husband and instructed him to use his "stern dad voice," (always more effective and scary than the stern mom voice), to tell the girls to turn off the TV, get the doll clothes off the dog and pour their Truth or Dare drink concoctions down the garbage disposal. It was 3:10 a.m. when I heard a noise outside the bedroom door. I opened the door and had to duck--three girls with painted faces turned on me, looking for the robber they just knew was lurking downstairs. One brave little soul held a plastic baseball bat aloft, one had a baton, and one was wielding an ominous bottle of shampoo, and was not afraid to use it!

The next night, after putting up with a cranky child who hadn't had enough sleep the night before, I was ready to conk out. Everyone was headed for bed when I heard the dreaded statement, "Mom, I don't feel good." Enter a night of sleeping on the recliner next to the couch-ridden sick child, waking every 45 minutes to check a fever, administer medicine, fluff a pillow, sing old Elvis tunes, turn cartwheels, whatever it took. And of course, even though he was better the next day, his fever came roaring back on Sunday night. This is because by the time you have a one-year-old you've learned that kids only get sick at night. And then THEY get to sleep the entire next day while you prop your eyelids open with toothpicks, and are forced to inject coffee directly into your veins.

Over the next five days we contended with one thing after another each night. Nightmares about going to school. Nightmares about NOT going to school. Too much caffeine: "Daddy let me drink a Mountain Dew. Is Daddy in trouble?" And of course, we had the inevitable: "I hear a noise. Can I sleep with you?"
Followed by: "My feet are cold."
Then: "My feet are hot."

And finally: "I can't feel my feet."

I was also cursed with non-children-related incidences that week. The dog got sick one night. There was a lonely cat with a blood-curdling screech howling in our backyard another night. And for good measure, we even had a horrendous wind storm that threatened to huff and puff and blow our house down.

By day seven, I couldn't take it any more. I called my sister and asked her if I could come to her house for the weekend and try to get some sleep.

All she has to deal with is a baby.

FEEDING FRENZY

Yesterday, as I stood over the stove boiling yet another pot of boxed macaroni and cheese to a mushy consistency (the way the kids like it) my mind wandered back to the days when I was pregnant with my firstborn. I had established firm plans regarding what, how and when my offspring would eat. This was before the four food groups got bored and morphed themselves into a much more hip food pyramid, but I was still quite certain what types of all natural and healthy food would be offered to my children and envisioned how they would gratefully enjoy it all. I knew this because I had *read all the books about it.* The experts TOLD me. All you have to do is introduce a multitude of tastes, textures and flavors when they start off on baby food. Strained beets? Center stage. Cottage cheese? On the menu frequently. Squash? Yes, even though it stained every bib in the house an ugly rust color. My husband and I lovingly prepared balanced meals for the first child, who was born weighing nearly 10 pounds and possessing a perpetually empty stomach. Vegetables were our friends, and mealtimes were pleasant, calm affairs.

Then came the second child.

Those of you with more than one child know what happens next. Although Baby Number Two was a beautiful infant with a sunny disposition, the sheer addition of another child to the family altered mealtimes dramatically. My rules loosened up and my expectations headed south, a little every year.

And now, nine years later, I am Queen of Processed Pasta, and toaster pastries are considered a staple food in our house. We now eat mostly what the kids like, mostly when they want it and mostly how they want it. And I am a lucky one. My cousin's kid eats only one vegetable: corn. And it must not be touching anything else on the plate or all bets are off. A friend of mine has been known to actually take her kid grocery shopping so he could be "more personally invested" in the mealtime preparation process, and therefore more likely to eat what she sets in front of him. This kid does a nice job of disproving all of those new-age approaches. It's Oreos, Oscar Meyer Hot Dogs and Fruit Loops for him every day.

The challenge isn't just finding something they like to eat. It's finding something they like to eat that can be made IN A HUGE HURRY. I am often found standing in front of an open refrigerator at 5:00 p.m., frantically searching the shelves for anything acceptable that takes less than 20 minutes to conjure up, while my children threaten to faint at my feet from hunger.

That doesn't mean I've stopped trying to be creative. Yesterday, as I assumed the position in front of the refrigerator, the cold air must have broken through to my nutrient-starved brain cells. I remembered: the latest edition of my "Busy Moms" magazine featured something called "Kitchen Cabinet" recipes. "Don't worry!" the article had said. "You can whip up these delightful meals from items you will find in your own cupboards." I raced for the magazine, rifled through the pages, and there they were--the recipes that would save me.

Now, for a brief moment, I smiled, headed back to the kitchen and started dreaming of the adoring exclamations that would emanate from my family members when they feasted their eyes upon my new creation. For a moment. And then reality set in, and I started to develop a pantry inferiority complex. The recipe was for Curried Chickpea Stew. Really! It was "this month's test-kitchen favorite!" It included things like two cloves of garlic, curry powder, peeled and minced fresh ginger root, actual CANS OF CHICK PEAS (RINSED AND DRAINED) and minced fresh parsley. As an option you could "make it even healthier by adding some chopped fresh spinach." Further down it casually mentions that you will have to remove two cups of the mixture at some point in the process and PUREE IT IN THE BLENDER UNTIL SMOOTH.

First of all, I don't think any recipe with a step including puree-ing counts as a quick meal. Second, I had none of these ingredients on hand and probably never would. OK, I could find the salt maybe, but that was about it. And third, no child in my universe would eat this stuff anyway. I checked the article headline again. Yes, it was the easy kitchen cabinet meals for busy families. All I can say is those test-kitchen people obviously do not have children because most parents understand that you really only put spinach on the table once, and then you never buy it again. And it is the rare child who would not look at a plate full of chick peas and immediately assume you have provided him with a fun new source of ammunition to use on his sibling across the table. These things would never find their way into my kitchen cabinet, much less my children's mouths.

I looked at the clock. It was 5:25 pm. The starving kids were beginning to salivate over the dog's bowl of kibble. I hurriedly flipped another page in the magazine, and found an ad for canned soup that outlined a four-ingredient recipe.

Ah, canned soup--something that truly does reside in my pantry. I stumbled to the stove and speed-cooked. The night's menu: Soup and something with macaroni and cheese.

My kids loved it.

SPURT ALERT!

It finally happened. I knew it was coming; it was only a matter of time. But I was still startled when, just a few weeks ago, I suddenly found myself looking UP into the eyes of my 14-year-old son. Up--not down, and not even straight into. UP!

This latest spurt should not come as such a shock to me. My husband and I have been tracking the kids' growth (and the dog's) on the bedroom door frame for quite some time. In fact, the door frame growth chart tells us that BOTH children have gained almost four inches in the past nine months (though thankfully the dog has stalled at 1'10"). My son has been impatiently waiting for the day when he could say he is taller than me. He now makes a point of swaggering by and *leaning* on my shoulder, calling me "shorty" and reporting on the status of my dark roots and gray hairs. He thinks this turn of events is just great.

I agree that there may be certain advantages to his new height. For example, I can now say to him, "Son! Change that light bulb over the sink!" and he can do it. I can also say to him, "Son! Reach up and water those hanging flower baskets on the front porch!" and he can do that too. I can even say, "Son! Let me know if the dust on top of the refrigerator has accumulated to the point where you can write your name in it!" and he will gladly oblige.

Still, for me, just the sound of the word "spurt" conjures up more negative thoughts than positive ones, like:
Spurt! His jeans are too short--again.
Spurt! His T-shirts show his belly.

Spurt! A big toe comes bursting through the end of a shoe.

Spurt! The grocery bill triples, and it takes two shopping carts just to hold the breakfast cereal needed for the week.

But what's worse, I am now left without one of my favorite weapons in the parental arsenal. It's a definite advantage when your children are shorter than you, the presumed authority figure. You are clearly the dominant force, the one who can peer down at them with that classic parental "look" and make your point in an unmistakable manner. Now that he can look down at the top of MY head, what do I do? Somehow, I think taking the time to pull out a stepstool before giving him an in-your-face lecture would lessen the desired effect.

I guess it's time to simply accept the inevitable: Even though I am 5'8", I will very soon be the shortest person in my family.

Good thing I still have the dog to boss around.

FLUNKING THE PARENTAL I.Q. TEST

I was once a smart person.

Not a genius, mind you, but a reasonably well-educated human being who possessed a respectable supply of common sense. Recently however, my I.Q. has been under fire. It seems now that my former 12-year-old child has morphed into a full-fledged TEENAGER, everything that comes from my lips must be questioned. Even the simplest statements need to be contested.

If I say it's time for bed, or that it's going to be cold so he needs a sweatshirt, or he can't keep those praying mantis eggs in the house, I get incredulous responses like, "Six a.m. isn't early!" "It won't get THAT cold!" and "It'll take at least four weeks for these cocoons to hatch!"

(I don't need to tell you what happened the next day. In the house).

Not only has my intelligence been dwindling, but apparently my organizational skills are on a rapid decline as well. In a recent 24-hour stretch, I was called upon to find the following missing items (all belonging to New Teenager) with disappointing results:

- The memory card from the last computer game New Teenager was playing (What's a memory card??);
- The gold soccer socks that New Teenager wore to practice last week and forgot to put in the wash;
- The library book New Teenager was reading in his tent four nights ago, before it rained.

Then there's my lack of judgment. I will not allow New Teenager to drive the car home from Grandma's, I will not allow New Teenager to watch R-rated movies and I will not allow New Teenager to surf the internet without supervision. In the world of Teens today, this kind of parental behavior is considered outrageous and a sure sign of dementia.

I sometimes have to remind myself that I have indeed slogged through many years of schooling--and I have the student loan payment books to prove it. I know who my government representatives are, I can figure out an algebra problem (as long as there is no time limit, of course) and I can even reset the clock on my VCR. Honest. But somehow, with the turning of a few calendar pages, I am now two bricks short of a load, a dim bulb, no smarter than a box of rocks.

After a particularly challenging day trying to prove to New Teenager that I still possess a few functioning brain cells, I turned to my husband, who has also recently been branded a dummy. "Will we ever be smart again?" I implored.

With great insight and intelligence he replied, "Sure. In about seven years."

FAMILY NIGHT FIASCO

A long time ago, probably when I was pregnant with my first child and the resulting hormonal imbalance had skewed my sense of reality, I read a parenting book that highly recommended that a family unit gather on a regular basis for "Family Nights." According to the expert author, these scheduled Family Nights would accomplish several things:

> 1. Family members would be able to "have a proactive dialogue" to air and resolve any "festering issues;" and/or
> 2. Members could participate in various "bonding" activities that would serve to bring the family closer together emotionally.

This sounds good on paper. And probably, most normal households would be able to pull it off. It just doesn't work at my house.

Here's a rendition of our most recent attempt at Family Night:

Mom: (*played by me, the long-suffering mother who merely wants to bring her family closer together emotionally*) Hey family members! How about we get together this evening for a Proactive Dialogue so we can air and resolve our Festering Issues?? I'll make some popcorn!

Dad: (*played by my husband of 20 years who should know by now that these kinds of suggestions are NOT really suggestions, rather they are COMMANDS thinly disguised as suggestions*) Uhhhhhh...I'm not sure I'll be around...and besides, the replay of the 1986

Masters Tournament comes on *The Golf Channel* at nine…

Teenage son: *(played by my teenage son, who only took the music player earphones out of his ears long enough to catch the word "popcorn" come out of my mouth)* Food?? Where???

Teenage daughter: *(played by my 13-year-old, whose social calendar rivals that of the entire British Royal Family)* Mom! You CAN'T be serious. I have Andrea at 6:00 for a phone consultation, then I'm supposed to be at Whitney's by 7:00 so we can walk over to Jacob's together at 7:30 for a movie that will last approximately 90 minutes. Then I need to be back home on the computer by 9:30 so I can Instant Message Andrea and Whitney about the movie. Then I need to shower and do my nails while I watch the 3rd show from the 4th season DVD of *Gilmore Girls*. I can't skip a night, or I'd have to start all over.

Me: *(now threatening to break out the sackcloth and ashes)* Oh come on, family members! This is our chance to bond! Can't we please carve out some time to discuss our personal challenges, review our family mission statement and set some goals for the next quarter??

Dad: *(still oblivious to the spousal "evil eye" being cast in his direction)* Uhhhhhh…does this involve talking? Because you really can't be having side conversations when you're watching The Masters…

Teenage son: (*putting the earphones back in his ears and sauntering to the kitchen with a frown*) I thought someone said there would be food.

Teenage daughter: (*heading toward the back door*) Can someone pick me up from Jacob's at 9:00? Can I borrow your flip flops, mom? Has anyone seen my cell phone? I gotta call Andrea and tell her to meet me at Whitney's...

In an instant, I was left standing in the living room with no one but Zoey, our Yellow Lab, who wagged her tail and promptly flopped onto her back so I could scratch her tummy.

That qualifies as bonding, doesn't it?

HOT ON THE TRAIL

I heard an interesting story on the news the other day. According to the report, we parents now have access to innovative new tracking devices called "Black Boxes" that we can secretly place inside our teenage son or daughter's car so we can always know their location. We can even use a remote control to make the car horn beep if they're driving too fast. We can also buy cell phones that will transmit a child's every move, or we may choose to sew a signaling mechanism in the collars of their school jackets. Some of these spy-world gadgets can cost over $1,000.

Personally, I don't get it. I do not need these high-tech tracking devices for my children. In fact, whenever I arrive home, I can tell you exactly what my offspring did all day long, without consulting any global positioning satellites or checking a monitor of any kind.

Yesterday, for example, I walked in the back door and promptly tripped over a pair of muddy size 13 cleats. Aha! Son obviously had soccer practice. A few steps further into the kitchen and my finely-honed detective skills kicked in once again. I concluded from the items on the kitchen counter that:

- For breakfast, Daughter enjoyed the middle sections only of two pieces of toast, along with a glass of chocolate milk;
- Son consumed one and a half giant bowls of Frosty Fruity-o's before deciding he was full;
- Lunch had consisted of several cans of soup, three apples and an entire package of hot dogs; and
- Someone tried to make a smoothie in the blender, using questionable ingredients.

I could tell by the looks of the laundry room that Son had to try on several outfits before settling on the perfect gym shorts and T-shirt combination. I could see that he also had some trouble finding a pair of gym socks and found it necessary to root through two baskets of folded clothes to hunt them down.

Cruising through the rest of the house, I began to piece together my daughter's activities. One look in her room and I figured out she had spent way too much time reading a book when she should have been cleaning. It was clear from the clothes and wet towels on the floor in my bathroom that she took a shower. And--judging from the Little Debbie Cosmic Brownie wrappers left as clues on my desk--someone was using the computer when she was not supposed to.

Now you might think I would be tempted to throw some kind of major hissy fit in reaction to this situation. Truth be told, the thought DID cross my mind, along with other thoughts that involved years of groundings and irrevocable servitude. But then I realized perhaps my thoughtful children were merely trying to SAVE ME MONEY by leaving a noticeable trail that left no doubts about their whereabouts. I failed to recognize the compassionate thoughts behind their behavior.

I guess when it comes to my teens, I will remain forever clueless.

THE SECRET LIFE OF LAUNDRY BASKETS

I have noticed a peculiar phenomenon in my utility room: the laundry baskets have all escaped and are now leading different, more interesting lives. They're supposed to be just plain old laundry baskets, dutifully collecting dirty clothes in each child's bedroom, then giving up that laundry to the washing machine and waiting patiently to be filled with clean clothes. Then they are to be transported upstairs to be emptied and filled with dirty laundry once again. That's it. But do they accept this fundamental role in life? No, not the laundry baskets in MY house. They refuse to be pigeonholed. They misbehave and chip away at my patience until I finally give up and let them go do something else.

The mischief begins when they start deploying a mysterious, Star-Wars-like force field around themselves--one so powerful that it prevents ANY DIRTY CLOTHES FROM BEING TOSSED INTO THEM. It's true. Right now, you could go up to my kids' closets and you will see for yourself that there is no dirty laundry in their baskets. Instead, the dirty clothes lay in rejected heaps, all around the basket. Sometimes, the force is so strong that the clothes aren't even in the closet at all--they have been catapulted clear across the bedroom, landing on the floor, the dressers or the top of the doors. Obviously, this is the work of some sinister force.

The baskets in my house also play mind games. They can make their owners THINK they have been emptied of clean clothes, as the mother in the house has requested, but as soon as your back is turned, poof! The clean clothes are back in the basket, as if THEY

WERE NEVER PUT AWAY AT ALL! It's just creepy. And the basket relegated to the chronic task of holding the slew of socks that need to be matched? I suspect it passively-aggressively eats every third sock in its possession, just to make trouble.

Some of our laundry baskets have been known to perform gymnastic feats in order to get our attention. Why, just this week my son complained that he had no clean underwear; and when I went into his closet to investigate, there were the laundry baskets, filled with clean clothes (including underwear), stacked THREE HIGH in a death-defying tower of defiance. How do they DO that??

Faced with this deviant behavior, I am obliged to let my laundry baskets pursue other interests.

In fact, in the past few years I have purchased 10 laundry baskets, of which at least nine have won the fight and have moved on to greener pastures. One now holds files in the basement, one holds newspaper clippings that will some day be pasted in a scrapbook (ha!), and one holds pool toys on the back porch. And there's that one basket that is reserved exclusively for my three-year-old niece to sit in and slide down the stairway steps.

I guess I can see their point--that does sound like a lot more fun than laundry to me, too.

RUDE AWAKENING

Something weird is going on in my house at bedtime: my children now go to bed later than I do.

Nothing, as far as I can tell, has changed for my husband and me. We are clearly aware of nightfall, and if for some reason we cannot see outside, we can tell by the hands on the clock when it's time to call it a day. Simple enough. Our children, however, have lost all ability to sense and/or plan for impending slumber. When I have hit the stage when I need to prop my eyelids open with toothpicks and my speech is slurring (approximately 9:30 p.m. most nights) the two teens in my house are just firing up their computers, calling their friends and opening the fridge for round two of the feeding frenzies that occur nightly. When I am flipping a coin to see if I will bother with the 10 minutes it takes to properly cleanse, hydrate and moisturize my face before bed or take a short cut by slap-dashing some warm water in the general vicinity of my face as I walk by the sink, they are just starting their homework. By the time I've changed into my pajamas and unearthed my slippers from the dog's stash of stolen goods under the bed, they are flipping on the TV to find the sports report. My husband will be snoring (despite the fact that he'll tell you he was really watching *The Golf Channel*, albeit with his eyes closed) when the kids are just cranking up their tunes on their ipods.

I know this is some kind of milestone in child-rearing, but I'm not sure how to take it. What is the explanation for such a turn of events?? Not so long ago, I was rocking these two babies to sleep at a mercifully early time such as 8:00 p.m., leaving me with at least two golden hours to pick up the house or watch a TV show that didn't feature a giggly puppet or an oversized purple dinosaur. In grade school, their bedtime was still a reasonable 9:00 p.m. Now, at 11:00 p.m. we can hear the shower running and the computer dinging when their friends log in to talk. They're revving up when we're winding down and I have to say, this disparity of our sleep cycles is getting a tad annoying.

They tell me they can't help it. It must be those wild and wonderful teenage hormones, or a growth spurt, or a caffeine jag, but they're just too wired to go to bed at a decent time. Instead of being concerned about this teenage phenomenon, perhaps I should learn to take advantage of their extended energy and assign chores to be completed while they're still up. One could do dishes, one could do laundry and they both could let the dogs out. And in. And back out. And back in. Think of all the work that could be done while I peacefully snooze! It would be like having the shoemaker's elves at my beck and call. I think I'll start implementing this new concept tonight.

I have a feeling that by tomorrow night, their insomnia will be cured.

SOMETHING BORROWED

Has anyone seen my:

- Round Hairbrush
- Gold Sandals
- Caribbean Breeze Nail polish
- Favorite Pen
- White Tank Top and
- Long Lash Mascara?

Actually, I don't need to issue an All Points Bulletin on these items. I already know where they are and who the culprit is. The borrower is someone who lives with me--my 13-year-old daughter.

I really can't figure this out. The problem is not that she doesn't have such things of her own. It's just that for some reason, even though I've been told by this same daughter that I don't dress "cool," my hair is very "90s" and I'm hopelessly "old-fashioned," my particular possessions cause some kind of mysterious temptation. This is especially true for objects on my bathroom vanity.

In fact, just this morning, I reached for my too-expensive salon brand hair spray, but it was gone. This constitutes an emergency for me, as it's the only chemical concoction I have found that will keep my hair from looking like a bale of straw by the end of the day. Where was it hiding? In teenage daughter's purse. And when I returned to the bathroom, I noticed my curling iron had also been confiscated. I had to resort to using her lukewarm Special Edition Mary Kate and Ashley Curling Iron as a back-up. And if you must know, the stubble on my legs today is a direct result of my razor being spirited out of my shower to some unknown destination.

There was a time when I looked forward to my little girl growing up--just think of all the clothes-and-shoe-sharing possibilities! Well, it didn't quite work out that way. Unfortunately, her shoe size and mine were the same for about five minutes, so except for the aforementioned sandals, we can not comfortably swap shoes. And I would look slightly ridiculous in one of her skinny little t-shirts that say things like, "I had a Nightmare I was a Blonde," especially since I regularly fork over fistfuls of cash for blonde highlights in my hair, not to mention the fact that I am not skinny.

"You're lucky teenage sons don't do this," I told my husband this morning as I was struggling with Mary Kate and Ashley and searching for my toothpaste. "Sons only eat and drink everything that's not nailed down."

He was about to agree when he opened the shower door and stopped in his tracks: "Has anyone seen my shampoo??"

THERE'S NOTHING TO EAT!

I won an award the other day, and I didn't even know I was in a contest.

It's not the kind of award where you end up standing on a podium, tears of joy streaming down your face as you wave to throngs of your adoring fans. It's not even the kind of award where you win money. In fact, it's quite the opposite. It's the kind of award that makes you blink several times and respond, in a less-than-thrilled voice: "Oh. That's just so great. Thanks for sharing that with me." Which is exactly what I muttered when the check-out lady at the grocery store loudly proclaimed to all within earshot that I had WON! I was the customer with the *longest cash register receipt that week*!

OK, so my grocery shopping trips are a tad out of control. Is that any reason to single me out? Surely there are other moms out there who have to rent a U-Haul, enroll in a strength training course and take out a personal loan every time they get groceries. Can I be the only one who takes a bungee cord to the store so I can strap two carts together to hold all the items on my list?   Doesn't anyone else find themselves threatening bodily harm when the store decides to move the aisles around just when you've honed your shopping time down to a mere four hours??

I remember the days when I could slip away and do my grocery shopping over a lunch break or on the way home from work. I would enter the store with a smile on my face, and leave less than an hour later with my smile, and checking account, still intact. Now however, I have to take a vacation day in order to get the groceries and another vacation day so I can *recover* from getting the groceries. This is because I live with two bottomless pits masquerading as children who eat twice their weight in food every 90 minutes. Like a swarm of locusts, they can make four gallons of milk disappear in half a day and leave only crumbs and crusts where once an innocent loaf of bread stood. When I return from grocery shopping, they morph into a pack of wolves, circling my van when it pulls into the garage, ripping into the grocery bags and eating the food before I can even put it away. And their vocabulary mainly consists of the following phrases:

"When are we going to eat?" and

"I'm starving!" and

"What's for (pick one) breakfast/lunch/dinner/snack?" and, after a three course meal,

"I'm still hungry. When are we going to eat again?"

Then there's the ultimate declaration, the one that can send me over the edge after a $300 shopping excursion: "There's nothing to eat around here!"

Apparently, I am no match for their chronically empty stomachs. But I'm not going to stop trying. And who knows, perhaps someday I'll perceive grocery shopping as an enjoyable experience once again.

There has to be an award for that.

THE RACE IS ON

I have a lot in common with Dale Earnhardt, Jr.

Well, except for the fact that he drives a race car and I drive a soccer mom van. And he wears high-tech jumpsuits with ads plastered all over them and I haven't worn a jumpsuit since my mom made one for me out of some hideous seersucker material when I was in the sixth grade. And, (and this is a BIG and) he makes about a zillion dollars more than me.

But aside from those differences, I think Dale and I could sit down over a cup of joe and find some common ground. For instance, like him, I also feel like I spend most of the day racing around in circles. I can relate to the frustration of having to fill up my gas tank every time I turn a corner. And I too sometimes have trouble hoisting a trophy in the air while waving to my adoring fans at the same time.

However, Junior and I just might get into a little tiff over whose driving experiences are more harrowing. He'll go on and on about how fast he has to drive, and how close the other cars get to his, and how long he has to be in that cramped, hot space. But I can counter with the fact that I regularly have to transport two children to two different destinations two miles apart with only two minutes to do so. Plus, to make it even more nerve-racking, my passengers are often arguing at decibel levels that can shatter glass, while all he has to contend with is the occasional crew chief voice in his ear suggesting he get new tires sometime soon.

His pit stops are short and sweet and everyone runs around doing everything for him while he probably just sits back and eats bonbons. My pit stops consist of flying into the gas station parking lot and commanding the passengers to jump out of the van and run at breakneck speed into the store, purchase the three critical fuel components necessary to make it through their day--a bag of Combos, two Mountain Dews and a Twix candy bar--and then head out the door without tripping, dropping any items or pausing for any unnecessary conversation. While this is going on, I get out of the van and brave the elements to pump only enough gas into my tank to successfully get me back home with my bank account still in the black.

His race includes some fancy maneuvering and vying for a top position among many other drivers. My race includes circling the school parking lot like a vulture until I spy a prime spot, making menacing faces to any and all oncoming drivers who might even think about taking the spot I've clearly put telepathic dibs on, then gunning my van in an intimidating manner as I roar toward my parking space.

His checkered flag moment comes when his car noses ahead of the rest of the cars and crosses the finish line first. Mine comes when my cargo has been safely delivered to their destinations and I have returned the van to the garage without the "Check Engine" light flashing in my face. Then he gets another trophy and great piles of cash, and I get to hop back in the van 30 minutes later to go pick everyone up.

At least I don't have to wear a jumpsuit.

TOP TEN SILLY QUESTIONS PARENTS ASK

Even though I've been a parent for 15 years, I am still slow to catch on to some important aspects of communication with my children. For example, it has only recently dawned on me that I have been asking my children extremely futile questions, and I should be wising up and completely eliminating these questions from my repertoire. As a public service to all parents out there, I offer the following personal list of TOP TEN SILLY QUESTIONS PARENTS ASK KIDS:

#10. What's that noise?

You almost never want to hear the answer to this question anyway, so why even ask? In the past, I have received such hair-raising responses as:

"What noise? We're just trying to teach the dog to run the vacuum cleaner."

and

"Oh, I threw Curtis's sock out the window and he's on the roof trying to get it."

And the most frightening response of all:

"Nothing..."

My suggestion? If you hear an unexplainable noise, just turn up the volume on your TV to drown it out and go about your business.

#9. Who did that?

Not even the top CIA agents in the country could get to the bottom of this question, so *you* should not even attempt to find out who left the milk out, who rooted through the clean clothes pile, or who left the front door wide open. Accept the fact that these will remain unsolved mysteries.

#8. Where's the (pick one) remote control/ cordless phone/scissors/hairbrush?

When you have children in the house, you will have perpetually missing objects, and you might as well get used to using a butter knife to cut coupons and actually getting up to change channels on the TV.

#7. How much will THAT cost?

Whatever you think "it" (ball uniform, school fees, lunch money for the week, or a birthday party with 20 of your kid's closest friends) should cost, just automatically double or triple that expectation and become good friends with your banker.

#6. Do you have your homework done?

Of course, the real answer is always no, so don't bother. And never, never, never ask this question after 10:00 p.m. unless you are prepared to hastily construct a model of the atom out of pipe cleaners and golf balls.

#5. Who called?

Here's a little-known scientific fact: Human beings under the age of 18 are physically and mentally incapable of finding a pen AND a piece of paper AND taking an understandable message from a phone caller because they are usually watching TV or talking to a friend on the other line and can't be bothered by such annoying interruptions.

#4. Is your room clean?

Yea, right.

#3. Can someone give me a hand here?

If you want to clear a room in my house, simply appear in a doorway struggling with heavy bags of groceries and ask for help. Long-lost co-inhabitants will only magically re-appear when they are hungry (and, oddly enough, the groceries are *put away*). Which leads me to...

#2. Are you hungry?

The answer to this question is always yes, no matter if it's 2:00 a.m. or you just finished a seven-course Thanksgiving Dinner.

And finally, the #1 Silly Question:
Is there really nothing on the calendar tonight??

Just when you thought it was safe to relax on the settee and have someone fan you while you nibble on grapes, you foolishly make this remark. What you will get in return is a litany of "Uh-ohs," "Oh-nos" and "Oops I forgots" that will result in a minimum of 17 trips to the store/the school/the gym and an overwhelming urge to pelt someone with those grapes.

Silly, silly me. I'll have to get to work and come up with more realistic questions to ask my children; ones that will actually provide me with useful responses.

Can someone give me a hand??

THE FORCE IS WITH ME

There's a mysterious, unearthly phenomenon at work in my home. I can't find a scientific name for it in any academic journal, but I know it exists because the evidence can be found at every turn. Household items are not being put where they should be put, and not one of the human beings who live with me can explain the situation. So I have come to the conclusion that my house must be possessed by an Anti-Order Force Field. That's right. It's a force so powerful it can move inanimate objects at will and it keeps my surroundings from being orderly and neat, as they should be.

Skeptical? Consider this:
In my utility room, where I wash clothes by the metric ton, there are two empty laundry baskets in the corner, surrounded by an array of dirty clothes *on the floor.* No one seems to know how this happens. Evidently, the sweaty basketball shirt, understanding its place, attempted to deposit itself into the laundry basket, only to be inexplicably HURLED BACK OUT! Same with the jeans and T-shirts lying in a defeated heap nearby. What other reason can there be? It's the Force Field, I'm sure of it.

Unfortunately, this sinister invisible barrier does not contain itself to a small area of the house. All of our closets contain piles of folded, clean laundry that resists any effort to deposit them on their proper shelves. The coat racks by the doors are uncovered, while the coats lie in a pile underneath, rejected. And lurking inside the toilet paper holder is the strongest of forces. While my spouse and children assure me that they ALWAYS change the roll when it's finished, I can walk into any one of our bathrooms and see the new roll perched precariously on top of the empty roll. This is clearly the work of some supernatural influence.

Pens and pencils float from the drawers where they are supposed to reside and end up on the floor, on the coffee table or on bathroom vanities. Shoes, instead of being content to stay in the cubby hole by the back door, are sneaking into the living room, hiding under the beds and joyriding in the car. Tape and scissors disappear altogether. The portable phone is barred from its base, and the gallon of milk is spirited from the refrigerator, ending up warm on a kitchen counter. The pets aren't spared either. The cats are to be fed twice a day, yet their bowl will sit unfilled; and the dog will bark to be let out, even though a child insists the dog was *just let out a few minutes ago*. It's just plain spooky.

My sole consolation is that I am not the only one who is bewitched by this extraordinary effect: "Where's the remote??" my husband bellows almost daily. I simply shrug.

The Anti-Order Force Field wins again.

DRIVING DAD CRAZY

Dear hubby,

I have noticed since our son turned 15 ½ and obtained his driver's permit that your health has suffered terribly. You have been more than a little tense, and dozens of new gray hairs have sprung up on your head. When you get in the passenger seat of our vehicle, your hands start to shake and your face develops a ghostly-white pallor. And your vocal chords are definitely strained from constant high-decibel outbursts such as "SLOW DOWN!" and "THAT'S A ONE-WAY STREET!" and "WE'RE ALL GOING TO DIE!!"

So, in the interest of your health, and our son's eardrums, I am providing the following guide:

***Instructions for the Father When Taking a
15 ½-Year-Old Child Out For Driving Lessons
in the Soccer Mom's Van***

Teaching your son to drive without having a breakdown *is* possible. It's really a matter of utilizing more constructive expressions and behaviors than those currently being used. For example, this is what you SHOULD say when he's not slowing to a stop: "Son, you might want to consider slowing down sooner. Those intersections come up rather quickly..." Rather than what you WANT to say, which is "Hey--Hello-o-o! That's a STOP SIGN up there! You're going to give us all whiplash!"

This is what you SHOULD do when he tries to change lanes in the middle of heavy traffic: Grit your teeth, bite your tongue and sit on your hands.

Instead of what you WANT to do, which is grab the wheel, stomp on the brakes and banish him to the back seat forever.

This is what you SHOULD say when he takes a curve too fast:
"Those yellow signs tell you the correct speed to take a curve, son. It's a good idea to pay attention and follow that state-sanctioned limit."
Not what you WANT to say, which is "Holy cow! You think you're Sam Hornish, Jr. in a NASCAR race?? Back it off!!"

And this is what you SHOULD tell him when you're finished with the lesson:
"You're getting better, son. Those children on the sidewalk were really overreacting."
Instead of what you WANT to tell him, which is "Take me to the ER!"

There are also a few calming self-talk phrases that you should repeat to yourself during these driving lessons in order to keep that vein on your forehead from popping out unnaturally:
    1.) This is only temporary;
    2.) I *will* live to see tomorrow; and
    3.) It could be worse. I could be shopping with my
        wife.

And honey, one last thing: never, ever dwell on the fact that we will soon have to purchase another car, our insurance rates are about to triple and having a teenage driver will add an entirely new category to our List of Things To Worry About.

Love,
Your Wife

P.S. Hope this helps, because guess what? Our daughter, the one who gets the brake and accelerator pedals confused, turns 15 ½ next year.

LOST IN TRANSLATION

Many years ago, I could ask my children questions or tell them to do something--and they would hear me, answer correctly, and happily do my bidding. Life was good, and except for that time when they asked the big, burly, tattooed man behind me in line at the grocery store why he had so much hair in his ears, I was mostly happy with our ability to communicate appropriately.

What I didn't realize was that at 12 years, 11 months and 31 days something weird would happen to them. At that point, a mysterious coating formed over the part of their brains that is in charge of hearing comprehension, congealed there like five-day-old-milk in a glass on my son's nightstand, and now prevents any parental communication from penetrating.

I like to call this condition *Hearing and Understanding now Halted*--or HUH? for short.

I have not seen much written in the medical journals about HUH?, but I can tell you from experience that there is no possible chance of successful interaction when teens are afflicted with it. Try as I might to be concise and informative in my messaging, things go unheard and undone.

One example of HUH? is the distorted translation of simple statements I make such as "Put your clothes away." This fairly innocuous command is converted by the teenage boy in my house to: "Take your neatly folded clothes and spew them in a disheveled manner all about your room, making sure that some objects fall haphazardly onto the floor where they will be crumpled and eventually coated with Labrador

Retriever hair, then pick the clothes up six days later, deem them unfit to wear and toss them back into the laundry."

When HUH? is in full swing, I can say things to my kids like, "Let the dog out," and 10 minutes later the dog will still be whimpering at the door with her legs crossed. I can say, "Rinse out your cereal bowl," and I will end up sandblasting rock-hard Cheerios from that same bowl. I can say, "Time to get up," and two hours later both children are still in lullaby land. Nothing gets through the HUH? filter!

Even written forms of communication are affected by HUH?. I once wrote the word "Vacuum" on a chore list I left for my teenage daughter when I went to work. I came home to find the house obviously un-vacuumed. Her reason? I had failed to specify WHAT was to be vacuumed, so my blatant lack of clarity resulted in a severe HUH? reaction.

Something must be done to combat this insidious ailment. Rather than go to all that trouble organizing a fundraising telethon or lobbying the drug companies to develop a pill that will clear the path from my mouth to their ears, perhaps I need to counter my kids' misinterpretations with a few select HUH? responses of my own, like when they want to use the car, stay out later or have some friends over.

I'm guessing a miracle cure for HUH? may be on its way.

BATTLE CRY

I have lost the Pop Tart battle.

Perhaps you were unaware that there was a serious tug-of-war going on between me and the corporate giant that produces toaster pastries. It's probably not headline news. However, since I became a parent, I have been staging an opposition against my children's consumption of high-sugar foods, and I was actually winning for awhile. When my oldest was five years old, his little friend asked him what his favorite Pop Tart flavor was. I'm not making this up--my son's reply was "What's a Pop Tart?" We were a fresh-fruit-and-whole-grains family, and I was determined to keep it that way.

Things have drastically changed. My once rigid rules about what my children would eat, drink and wear have gone by the wayside, abandoned like an overripe banana on our kitchen counter. Now, toaster pastries are considered a staple food and are on the breakfast menu for my teenagers almost every day. And they're not even the kind of tarts containing a smidgen of fruit that would slightly lessen my guilt and perhaps even my dentist bill. No, the latest craving is something mimicking campfire s'mores, with artificial marshmallows mixed with artificial chocolate fudge and topped with a layer of artificial frosting. The Pop Tart Defeat is merely symbolic of the overall loss of control I have suffered the past few years. At this point, I can confidently say Lay's potato chips, Frosted Flakes and Mountain Dew have joined Pop Tarts as the four main food groups in our house.

I have gone soft in other areas too. Evening routines were once predictable and, well, routine. Homework, bath times and bedtimes were on a tight schedule that ended promptly at 9:00 p.m. with a quiet reading period. There were no distractions of TV, computers, cell phones or music. Now in order to get their homework done, my kids must be simultaneously listening to their ipods, chatting on the computer and watching TIVO'd versions of *Kyle XY*. At 11:00 p.m. With a Mountain Dew.

There was also a time when I had no concern for what they wore because I was in charge of their wardrobe. Their clothing was neat, ironed and color coordinated. Now, if I suggest ironing something, I get laughed at and am reminded that it's cool to look like they've just rolled out of bed. The holes and rips in the jeans and shirts make them look like they've had a run-in with a swarm of moths. Don't even ask how many times their grandmothers have offered to mend the clothes that they paid too much money to look precisely that way.

It's my fault. I'm the one who waved the white flag and surrendered on these issues. I could only hold out for so long. I tell myself I'm simply picking my battles and saving my energy to tackle new, more important rules on subjects such as dating, use of the car, curfews and body piercings…

Besides, I have discovered the Brown Sugar Cinnamon Pop Tarts are really kind of tasty.

PETS ARE PEOPLE TOO

At some point years ago, perhaps back when I was recovering from having my wisdom teeth gouged out and didn't know my own name when I came out of surgery, I consented to have pets in my home. I want to caution those of you who have not yet made that fateful decision, to think twice.

I know, I know. Pets are supposed to add to our feeling of well-being and comfort. They add years to our lives, teach children responsibility, shower us with unconditional love, etcetera, etcetera. This is all well and good, if the pets happen to clearly understand their role and behave in a manner befitting domesticated animals. My pets don't follow those traditional rules of conduct. And to make matters worse, they are all suffering from identity crises.

Right now, as I write this, there is a 20-pound male cat outside the window behind me, begging to come in. He is not meowing politely, as if to say, "Won't you let me in, dear lady of the house?" No, he is on his hind feet and PUNCHING the window with both front paws in rapid succession, as if to say, "You bunch of idiots, let me in or else!" This from a cat that was rescued as a scrawny lost kitten and lovingly christened Tina by my daughter. I'm thinking he's paying us back for naming him something not appropriate for his gender. His twin brother Kelly (also named by my daughter) is just as warped. He sleeps in the dog kennel and eats only dog food.

At my feet, as I write this, is a senile cocker spaniel who cannot see or hear much and commences barking at the walls at exactly 7:25 p.m. every evening until he tuckers out around 9:00 p.m. He eats only cat food. And Oreo cookies.

In the living room, asleep with her paws in the air, is a two-year-old Yellow Lab who was supposed to be an outside dog. She knows 14 tricks, catches frogs in our pond, and will sell her soul for the cocker spaniel's Oreo cookie. When it became apparent that she would not have to be an outside dog, she decided she should sleep under our bed every night. This was not a problem when she was a puppy. Then as she grew into a hulky dog and could no longer scamper under the bed, she would lie on her side, grab the bed frame and drag herself under the bed. You can imagine what shape the dust ruffle was in after months of dog sliding abuse. We banned her from the room. Now she sleeps with my son. In his bed. Under the covers. With her head on a pillow.

In the kitchen is a blue parakeet named Max who detests any bird toys and promptly dismantles them whenever anyone attempts to hang one in his cage. He thinks he's a rooster, and screeches every morning at the crack of dawn. His favorite trick is to whistle for the Lab in the exact way that I do it. This was funny the first few times, then even the Lab got tired of running to the kitchen in response to the false alarms.

We have been through a line-up of pets in the last 20 years, the list growing more peculiar as my children grew older. There were salamanders named Slimy and Grimy, and a field mouse that lived in a coffee can. Last summer we nurtured an orphaned baby bird named "Lucky," who ultimately wasn't. We've had a collection of very boring hermit crabs, and cocoons of butterflies and praying mantises. We've taken in a crying kitten from the nearby bean field, a roving mutt from who-knows-where, and two county fair goldfish who refused to die for three long years. It's like living in the Central Park Zoo.

Now my son says he wants chickens, and my daughter insists that our back yard is plenty big enough for a horse.

I sure hope I will not be under the influence of any anesthesia in the near future...

YOU MIGHT BE THE PARENT OF A TEENAGER IF...

Though I have only been living with teenagers for three years and am in no way an expert on adolescents, I have learned a thing or two about the metamorphosis from innocent "tween" to full-blown teen status. It can be a subtle shift, a change that sneaks up on you without advance notice. But there are some clear warning signs that signal you are now living with a teen. As a public service, I am offering the following easy assessment tool for any parent to use if for some reason you are not sure you have become the parent of a genuine, bona fide teenager.

You might be the parent of a teenager...
...If you spend more money every month on groceries, mainly consisting of Pop Tarts, frozen pizza, Ramen noodles, Doritos and chicken pot pies, than the Gross National Product of several third world countries;
...If you attempt to open the door to your child's room and your entry is blocked by a mountain of wet bath towels;
...If you have suddenly lost all ability to make sense, your IQ has dropped dramatically and at times your attempts at civil conversation are considered so lame that you deserve only an eye roll in response.

You might be the parent of a teenager if you have to fight for time on your own computer.

You might be the parent of a teenager if your makeup, hair brushes and hair spray regularly disappears. Even if you only have sons.

You might be the parent of a teenager if your car's gas tank is perpetually on empty and the car can probably drive itself to the gym, the school and the pizza place automatically.

If you have recently purchased any electronic item that starts with a lower case "i"; had to ask someone to explain what the initials BRB, LOL and TTYL mean; bought three pairs of tennis shoes in three different sizes in one year for the same child; and you hear a "cha-ching" sound in your head and automatically reach for your wallet whenever they approach, you might be the parent of a teenager.

You might be the parent of a teenager if you can't get your kids to go to bed at night or get up in the morning; the decibel level for simple questions such as "Do we have any milk?" rivals that of the landing strip at O'Hare airport; and you have often chosen to completely discard an item of clothing that has resided in the dark, dingy corners of a gym bag for far too long rather than let it contaminate an entire load of wash.

This is not an all-inclusive list, of course. But, if you now feel compelled to cut out this article and hang it on your refrigerator door, amidst *Zits* cartoons, orthodontist appointment cards and the outrageous car insurance bill, well, congratulations my friend.

You truly are the parent of a teenager.

THROWING IN THE TOWEL

I found a cryptic note in the laundry room the other day, pinned haphazardly to a well-worn bath towel on the floor. It said: "Dear lady of the house--I am your towel. And I'm throwing myself in."

I couldn't believe what I was reading! My towels and I have been together for a long time; a few have actually been with me since the beginning of my wedded bliss 21 years ago. What would cause my beloved towel to give up a life of luxury in our home, I wondered? Why would one of these friends of the family, a dependable and loyal worker, ever consider abandoning its pampered life with us?

The note continued: "I signed on to perform standard functional duties as a bath towel in a normal household. I fully expected to be utilized once a week, washed and dried appropriately and returned to my safe haven in the linen closet."

Uh oh. Something must have happened to push my towel over its frayed edge. I recalled one incident where *perhaps* the towel was used to wipe muddy dog paws. Could that be it?

I read on: "The terms of my contract with the Weisenburger Household have been violated egregiously. My daily work load has increased exponentially, and the duties I now perform are completely outside of my original agreed-upon job parameters."

OK, I did once find that towel in the flowerbed. And I'm thinking that was the same towel that my son kept for several weeks in the trunk of his car where it proceeded to grow Penicillin cultures. And there *was* the time when the toilet in the guest bathroom overflowed and we used the towel (along with several throw rugs and some nearby curtains) to frantically stem the rising floodwaters...

There was more: "You are therefore notified that I am on strike and will not be returning to my duties unless and until the following demands have been met:

1.) My transportation route will consist only of round trips from the closet to the laundry room and back to the closet shelf. No detours to the teenage daughter's bedroom floor will be tolerated (although I do enjoy the camaraderie with the other six towels there).

2.) The teenage son may not use me as a napkin at the dinner table. I still have spaghetti sauce stains from the last time.

3.) Let's agree: Bath towels do <u>not</u> make good bird cage liners, oven mitts or campfire extinguishers. Need I say more?"

Then there was the final, devastating blow: "If these demands are not met, I will be forced to retaliate by sneaking Kleenexes into every washer load with me."

Clearly, I have been remiss and should negotiate a new contract with my towel. I should pledge to make its life more predictable, to use it only for the specified purposes and to never again abuse it under any circumstances.

But instead, I'll probably just go hide the box of Kleenex.

TIME TO EAT

Newsflash for Ripley's Believe It Or Not:
You may not consider this front page news, but to me, it's a rare and remarkable occurrence. I, a mother who made a simple New Year's Resolution to have more family dinners at the kitchen table, actually corralled all four family members on the same day at the same time in the same house at the same table for a somewhat civilized dining experience on Monday, April 14, 2008 at approximately 6:21 p.m.

At first, I didn't think I could pull it off. We gathered in January and flipped through the calendar pages searching for an evening, any evening, when my hyper-scheduled husband and two teenagers and I would potentially be home at the same time. Four months into the calendar, we thought we might have found one day when there would perhaps be a few minutes when it was possible that the stars would be aligned just right and our paths could cross. Maybe.

We circled the date in red. As it drew nearer, I took the necessary steps to ensure the success of our Dine Together Day:

• On DT-Day Minus Five, I polled the kids to see what they would like for our special dinner. That didn't work well because they couldn't name a meal that did not come in a McBox or McBag. I vaguely recalled a recipe from when I used to cook and headed to the grocery store, where I was heralded with balloons and a marching band after spending the equivalent of one child's college savings fund to appropriately stock our shelves.

- On DT Day Minus Four, I sent reminder memos to my children.

- On DT-Day Minus Three, I realized my children would not understand an actual paper memo so I had to learn how to send text messages to their cell phones. LOL.

- On DT-Day Minus Two, I started worrying that someone would call a last-minute practice or a mandatory meeting, so I rented a skywriting plane and flew over the town, leaving an unmistakable message in the clouds that went something like, "The Weisenburgers WILL eat together Monday at 6:15. No excuses."

- On DT-Day Minus One, I petitioned Congress to make April 14th a national holiday, allowing me sufficient time off to clear the kitchen table of credit card offers, expired coupons and Christmas cards from 2006.

- On DT-Day, I locked the doors, drew the shades and dispatched a SWAT Team to keep any unwanted intruders from thwarting my plan.

Miraculously, it happened. For 19½ minutes, the four of us were face to face around the table. We ate, we laughed, we remembered each other's names. And then, like firefighters responding to a four alarm fire, two jumped up to head to the gym, one sprinted for music lessons, and I was left alone at my seat, wishing I had taken photos to capture the historic moment.

After all, some stories are just too far-fetched for even Ripley's to believe.

ROAD TRIP REVISITED

When I was a little girl, our family took a two-week camping trip to Yellowstone National Park in Wyoming. I recall that vacation fondly, even though when I brought it up my mom started to shudder and mumbled that the station wagon radiator overheated every 30 minutes, we four kids fought non-stop (and one of us threw up out the car window), prairie dogs made off with all our food and my brother got lost in the Badlands of South Dakota. I sure didn't recall any of that. I thought the long hours on the highways seemed short as we passed the time singing rollicking versions of 99 Bottles of Beer on the Wall, logging state license plates and counting cows in the fields. I'm positive that we got along perfectly, and everyone enjoyed every minute together. I suggested to my mom that her recollection might be a tad skewed.

Awash in nostalgia, I eagerly made plans for a similar trek to Yellowstone with my husband and kids. I fantasized it would go something like this:

We would all pile into our vehicle, happily anticipating 10 days of carefree living together on the road. There would be no arguing, no complaining, and no battles over cup holders or armrests. We would enjoy long conversations about such things as religion, the subprime mortgage lending crisis and global warming. We would also spontaneously stop whenever we spotted an historic or educational site, and the children would be forever grateful for this life-changing experience.

Here's the way it really went:

- For the first 100 miles we chatted with each other, as I was strictly enforcing the rule of No Electronics. Everyone looked out the windows contentedly, and I think someone even made a comment about global warming (though looking back on it, it may have been a veiled complaint about the air conditioning).
- For the second 100 miles we counted cows, logged license plates and sang 99 Bottles of Beer on the Wall. Five times. Then my daughter slugged my son for using her cup holder.
- Somewhere between miles 200 and 500, I completely disregarded my own No Electronics rule in order to drown out the sounds of my kids fighting and my husband threatening to "turn this car around!"
- From miles 500 to 1500, no one spoke a word. In fact, we were totally oblivious of each other while we played with our own cell phones, laptops, videogames and DVD players. We stopped only to sleep, visit the World's Largest Frying Pan and view a Sacred White Buffalo that turned out to be a small bison with a skin condition.

We finally arrived in Wyoming for four fabulous days in the National Parks. But then…we had to drive back home. When we pulled into our driveway after 4,000 miles, battered and road-weary, and I was facing 10 days' worth of dirty laundry, there was only one thing left to do.

I called my mom. And I apologized. Profusely.

GREEN TEENS

The teenagers in my house are very environmentally-conscious. I know this because they are extremely picky about certain resources they use at home and are often staging silent protests against the misuse and overuse of such resources. In fact, they can be so passionate about their ideals that they refuse to properly utilize some material goods altogether.

Take, for example, the bathroom towel bars. For some reason, these racks are shunned by my green teens as a shameful waste of wood and wrought iron. Because of my kids' high regard for the limited assets of mother earth, every towel bar in the house sits lonely and perpetually unadorned by their towels, while every bathroom floor is littered with wet mounds of them.

Milk glasses are another limited natural resource that must be conserved, according to my kids. They are simply doing their part by drinking straight from the milk jug and not creating yet another dirty glass for the human race to deal with.

They also regularly take a stand against the use of plastic materials that clog our landfills, particularly if that plastic is shaped like a laundry basket and is supposed to contain their dirty clothes.

And then there's the shoe shelf at the back door. It's designed to neatly hold 10 pairs of teen shoes. Know how many are in there? Two. And they're mine. Apparently the shoe shelf is blacklisted, probably due to the remote possibility that it was made with wood from the dwindling Amazon rainforest.

The kids explain that refrigerated items are regularly left out on the kitchen counter because of their concern that opening the refrigerator door will harm the ozone layer. And as for cleaning supplies--the kids shout in alarm and back away whenever they come within five feet of them due to the alleged levels of harsh chemicals involved. Never mind that they sleep every night in bedrooms the EPA should add to their list of toxic dump sites.

When I questioned my children's logic and their interpretation of environmental commitment, they confronted me with my own brazen lack of awareness. They pointed out my wall calendar system with the matching bulletin board, meant to completely coordinate and synthesize family schedules and also serve as a handy place for important school papers. It currently holds a faded note about my daughter's preschool play and a vet appointment card for our dog Tyler...the one who died four years ago. They also accused me of owning a sewing machine that never gets utilized and they insisted it should be recycled. OK, yes, I probably would recycle it if I could find it.

Well. After *that* humbling discussion, I decided to make some drastic changes. My children's attitude did force me to re-evaluate and eliminate several things in particular that are just laying around the house and not simplifying my world at all. I just hope I didn't throw out anything valuable by mistake...that would be too bad, wouldn't it, kids?

Kids? Uh oh...Kids??

EIGHT SIMPLE REQUIREMENTS FOR DATING MY DAUGHTER

(with a wink and a nod to author W. Bruce Cameron)
In a few months, my daughter will be 16 and officially allowed to date. This situation is causing an inordinate amount of consternation for my husband and me. We are new to this sort of thing, and have been struggling to find a way to gently communicate to interested young men that our daughter is the precious apple of our eyes, and anyone who harms her in any way will meet with painful and tortuous consequences. Therefore, we are offering this list of helpful "interview" hints for the boys who are waiting in the wings, to ensure that expectations are met, intentions are clear and any intimidating weapons remain securely locked in our safe.

1.) Boys who drive a vehicle that would be described as a vehicle in name only, i.e. boys who drive conversion vans, monster trucks or clown cars, need not apply.

2.) Boys who show up at the door in questionable clothing would be wise to retreat. This is not a democratic process. Anyone appearing in chains, sporting longer hair than our daughter or openly displaying his preference for boxers or briefs will not be considered a viable candidate.

3.) Body piercings and/or tattoos are subject to intense scrutiny. Boys with optional decorations of this type must realize that the father in this equation still considers tattoos completely pointless and earrings solely a woman's accessory. As a result, an uncomfortable line of questioning *will* be thrust upon you.

4.) You will be asked what you want to be when you become an adult. If the answer contains any reference to "mime," "online gamer," or "Chippendales," you will be abruptly excused.

5.) If you already ARE an adult, do not pass Go and do not collect $200. Go directly to jail.

6.) If you have an unusual aversion to eye contact, even if due to typical teenage angst, it will be assumed that you are guilty of some type of immoral infraction and you will not be given an opportunity to prove your innocence.

7.) Be prepared to recite the Ten Commandments from memory, pass an extensive vocabulary quiz that will <u>not</u> include the words "freakin'," "dude" or "awesome" and demonstrate your ability to correctly utilize the terms "please," "thank you," and "Yes, sir. I will have her home by 11."

8.) And finally, if you meet all of the above criteria, a formal paper application will be required before any initial contact can be made with said daughter. Requested application information will include: General demographic statistics such as your Name, Date of Birth, Height, Weight, Driver's License Number, GPA, Boy Scout Rank, IQ, and list of any brushes, near-brushes, or confirmed brushes with the law.   In addition, the application must be accompanied by a complete financial statement, your unblemished employment history, an updated medical file and glowing references from your minister/pastor/priest, plus a full diagram of your family tree, which cannot be circular in nature.

Thank you for your interest. Please allow four to six years for processing.

THE HOLIDAYS: Going Overboard

THE MOST FRIGHTENING HOLIDAY

Halloween. The mere mention of the word sends shivers down my spine. It's not for reasons you might think, however. I can take the scary movies, the vampire stories, even black cats crossing my path. The notion that really strikes fear in my heart, makes my blood run cold and my knees go weak? Producing Halloween costumes. That's right. I'm a grown woman who is decidedly costume-challenged. For those of us suffering with this malady, there is no more frightening holiday tradition than dressing up our children for trick or treat.

I know there are those of you out there who relish the thought of creating awesome, prize-winning costumes every year, starting November 1st while your ideas are still fresh. I am related to some of you. But I do not share that particular gene. As the Halloween season approaches, and my children start talking about What They Want To Be, I know I will once again have to break their treat-loving hearts. Every year I must remind them that:

a. Their mother cannot sew. In fact, replacing popped buttons can sometimes take months and involve search parties for needles and thread, not to mention the occasional band-aid. And--
b. Their parents did not win the lottery or the Publisher's Clearinghouse Sweepstakes and are thus not blessed with loads of discretionary cash with which to buy the $199.99 latest fad costume with the flashing lights and holographic effects.

It doesn't even help if I start early. Last year, trying to beat the Bad Mother rap, I clearly discussed costume expectations with my children, beginning in early

September. It was settled: one bug, one princess. With ample preparation, I thought, and armed with my trusty stapler and double-sided tape, I could master these requests. Time was on my side. Until October 30th, when the bug request changed to a wizard request. I went desperately foraging for my graduation gown and ran out to buy yards of accent material that looked remotely wizard-ish. It was all destined to be stapled, taped and pinned together within an inch of its life.

A friend of mine was similarly lulled into the costume comfort zone one year, thinking she had it all under control. Suddenly, three days before Halloween, her seven-year-old decided that absolutely nothing but an Elvis costume would do. Wild attempts were made to secure the elusive costume, and several less-than-honorable store owners were threatened along the way. Finally, with only hours to spare, my frazzled friend produced a dazzling pint-sized Elvis costume, complete with sequins and guitar. "Thank God for charge cards and the internet," she muttered as he took his place in the costume contest parade, amid oohs and aahs from his admiring friends. She is seriously considering a written contract with her children that will contain a clause stating no costume changes after October 1st.

This is the kind of craziness that has lasted for generations in this country. When I was a child, I was once hastily dressed as some kind of water-repellent chicken (chicken mask, yellow raincoat, red glove for a tail). And I know my oldest brother once went as a four-course Thanksgiving dinner. The thought of that one still makes my mom twitch, 40 years later.

I know women who save lives on a daily basis, but crumble at the thought of putting together Halloween costumes. Why do we do this to ourselves, all for a measly two-hour event in our lives? Isn't there a better way?? I am waiting for my friends and colleagues to take me up on the idea of a Halloween costume exchange, like folks do for prom dresses. Bring in the costume your kid refuses to wear two years in a row, and exchange it for one my kid refuses to wear two years in a row.

Sounds good to me. But just in case, I'm going out to buy more staples.

HOLIDAY HALLUCINATIONS

It's that time of year again. The fall décor gets pushed aside by all things red and green, the holiday music kicks in over PA systems everywhere, and the gift catalogs jam the mailboxes. And I, as I do every November, get overtaken by a rush of sentimentality and initiate grandiose plans to create lovely and personal gifts for everyone on my Christmas list.

Let's see. Will I make some aromatic homemade candles this year? Yes! I'll buy some scented oil and wax tomorrow. What about the pretty layered brownie mixes in quart jars, all tied with ribbon and a hand-stenciled recipe card? They'll be great gifts for the teachers. And as soon as I can, I need to cut and dry the perennials from my flowerbeds, so I can make beautiful wreaths and pressed flower arrangements for my sisters.

There's just one problem with all this: I am not what you would consider a domestic goddess. I rarely bake, unless you count Pillsbury Cinnamon Rolls on Sunday mornings. When my kids need something sewn, they know they have to call Grandma. I don't even own a sewing machine. And my attempts at anything craft-y usually end up in the garbage can. I was just not blessed with those skills. But still…

I can't stop myself. There's something uniquely motivational about the holiday season. All those home and garden shows touting the many ways you can decorate a home using only pine cones and berries are enough to rouse my usually-dormant homemaking genes from their deep sleep. The magazine covers shout at me to bake seven kinds of cookies and share them with my neighbors at a cookie swap. I MUST cut real greens from a nearby woods to bring the authentic smell of Christmas to my home. And that nativity scene hand-carved out of soap doesn't look too tough to handle, does it? My children scatter when I start posing these questions and my husband suspects I've been prematurely nipping into the eggnog. They try to talk me out of it, but it's too late. I am in a holiday planning frenzy and have already purchased yards of raffia ribbon and brown paper that I can hand stamp for gift wrap.

Now, I know in my head that most of these projects will remain undone. It will get to be December 23rd, and with the clock ticking away, I will resort to gift certificates and overnight deliveries from giftcardsforprocrastinators.com to round out the gift list. The raffia and quart jars will be stored in a basement cabinet, right next to last year's "'Twas the Night Before Christmas" cross-stitch undertaking and the unfinished manger made entirely of dogwood twigs. But in my heart, I know I am creating something more: a genuine sense of anticipation and joy that comes from thinking about the ones I love and the many reasons I have to be thankful. And that's enough.

Except for maybe a pan or two of homemade fudge…

THE PLIGHT BEFORE CHRISTMAS

'Tis the month before Christmas and all through
the house,
Our two teens leave gift lists for me and my spouse.
They scribble and write, compose and compare,
In hopes that St. Nick has some big bucks to spare!

But Dad with his wallet and I with my purse,
Realize things have taken a turn for the worse.
Their lists once contained things that we could afford,
But as they have grown, so the prices have soared!

Tinker Toys and Legos have all been replaced,
And items like Play Doh are simply erased.
Where once there was Elmo, and Big Bird and Pooh,
There's now a cell phone, and an ipod too.

Gone are the days of toy cars and doll beds,
When visions of sugarplums danced in their heads.
Now they dream of two laptops (one's hers;
one's his)
And something called a jump drive--
Who knows what that is?!

It's CDs, and sweaters, and watches and rings,
Computer and Play Station games of all things.
A DVD burner will do just the trick,
Do they think money grows on trees for St. Nick??

More rapid than reindeer the items ring up,
We'll have to get second and third jobs to keep up!
The deadlines draw nearer, the panic sets in,
I won't get it all done! Where do I begin?!

Away to the bank I will fly like a flash,
To get an infusion of much-needed cash.
And what to my wondering eyes should appear,
But a bottom line that's already too bottom-near.

There's a twitch in my eye and an ache in my head,
Will my checkbook emerge alive, or dead?
Which things do I get, for whom and how many?
Excess cash? I sure don't have any!

So I think for a minute, and then start to smile--
The answer's been with me, there all the while.
I take a deep breath and I slow myself down;
I cancel more plans to go into town.

Then I gather my children and with hugs and a kiss,
I remind them it's not about presents and lists.
It's about friends and family, and laughter and love,
And the blessings we're given from God up above.

No matter what's wished for or what gifts are sought,
Christmas is not about things that we've bought.
In the midst of the frenzy and the lure of the mall,
We shouldn't forget...*the greatest Gift of all.*

So our presents get pared down to just two or three,
We'll wrap them with love and place them under
the tree.
And then I'll exclaim 'ere I turn in for the night,
"Happy Christmas to all, and...
                    ...*may we all get it right!*"

SOCK IT TO ME SANTA

Dear Santa,

All I want for Christmas is two matching socks.

I realize in the grand scheme of things, matching socks should not be a high priority. Socks are a staple item, a commodity that everyone needs and everyone buys without much thought. After all, they go on your feet and cover your *toes*--a decidedly unglamorous part of the human body. In my opinion, socks simply serve a bland, functional purpose and should go about their business in an orderly fashion with no questions asked.

Before we had children, our socks did just that. They paired up, stayed in neat rows in our drawers and never requested any furlough privileges. Aside from the fact that I never understood why a sock size is different than a shoe size for the very same foot, I had no quarrels with socks. But that is not the situation in my house currently. These days, the socks that come to live in my home turn into renegade free spirits, running amok and refusing to comply with basic sock rules of behavior. They have an alarmingly high divorce rate: they reject their partner and go solo after only a single wearing. They mix and mingle, disappear from sight for long periods of time, and jump mysteriously from our drawers to the floors of our children's rooms. And when the prodigal socks finally do return to our dressers, IF they return, evidence of their escapades is clear. They are stained with the kind of color that can only be described as Backyard Dirt, or they are permanently infused with Teenager Gym Bag Odor. And so, sadly, despite the fact that my husband and I have purchased 35 pairs of new socks in the past two months, we never have a decent matching pair in our possession.

We need to remedy this mess, and soon, because the socks are getting bolder by the minute. Several have recently been spotted in the van, on the patio and even in the dog kennel. And just last week the mother of my daughter's friend said she found one of my daughter's socks *lying in her driveway*. She lives three miles from our home.

We try to corral the errant socks in a laundry room basket all their own, where they can socialize to their hearts' content. But they continue to revolt. Any time my daughter attempts to put them together, blue dress socks somehow end up folded with the black ones and booty socks are mismatched with mid-calf length socks. Scary. And my son's socks have learned to cleverly dive completely out of sight at the bottom of the basket so he is constantly forced to use his dad's socks instead, even though his feet are two sizes larger. It's just inexplicable.

So Santa, if the elves have made some extra socks this year, I would sure appreciate a pair or two. Just don't plan on leaving them in my Christmas stocking.

I may be wearing it…

THE TWELVE DAYS OF CHRISTMAS VACATION
I save vacation days every year so that during the
holiday season, I am able to spend wonderful bonding
time with my children who are on Christmas break
from school. At least that's the way I imagine the
scene for 11 months and two weeks. And then reality
sets in, right around the day after Christmas.
If this year is anything like past years, here's how it
will actually sound:

(Sung to the tune of The Twelve Days of Christmas)

On the first day of Christmasvacation my teens will
hear from me--
"Let's have some family bon-ding."

On the second day of Christmasvacation my teens
will hear from me--
"Please make your beds...
Then we'll have a little family bon-ding."

On the third day of Christmasvacation my teens will
hear from me--
"Wash up your dishes,
Please make your beds...
And if time we might do family bon-ding."

On the fourth day of Christmasvacation my teens will
hear from me--
"What is that I smell?
Clean out your gym bags!
And don't forget again--
Put your wet tow-els in the laun-dry."

On the Fifth Day of Christmasvacation my kids won't
give to me--
FIVE MINUTES OF PEACE!
"Stop your bickering!
No more fights!
Go to bed it's 2 a.m…
But first put wet tow-els in the laun-dry!"

By the Sixth Day of Christmasvacation my teens will
give to me--
No response but eye-rolls
Not a Minute-of-Peace!
Four migraine headaches
Three gray hairs
Two Tylenol PM…
(But still no wet tow-els in the laun-dry!)

On the Seventh Day of Christmasvacation my teens
will hear from me--
"Hand over your cell phones!
No more computer!
I need Five-Minutes-of-Peace!
Your showers take too long
No more requests for cash
Maybe get a job…
And put your wet tow-els in the laun-dry!"

On the Eighth Day of Christmasvacation my teens
will hear from me--
"I say bonding-shmonding
Go do something somewhere
Get out of my hair
I need Five-Minutes-of-Peace!
Turn that music down
I can hardly hear

I'll shout this one more time:
Put your WET TOW-ELS in the LAUN-DRY!!"

The rest of Christmasvacation my teens will hear
from me--
"No more sleeping in!
This is not a hotel!
Pick up after yourself!
I am not your maid!
I-need-to-count-to-FIVE!
Whose idea was it
Giving 10 days off??
You're both grounded for life...
And tell your dad that he's doing laun-dry."

On the Last Day of Christmasvacation my kids will
hear from me--
"Pack up your book bags
Get lunch money ready
Finish all your homework
Get to bed early
Take a vitamin
Everyone is going
Back to school tomorrow
No ex-cuse allowed!
What's that? Yes I am
Smiling once again
I know it won't be long...
'Til there's an end to this family bon-ding!

RESOLUTION EVOLUTION

The new year arrived a few short months ago, and like most people, I made several resolutions to mark the occasion. Some of these resolutions may sound familiar to you. They sound familiar to me only because I have pretty much declared the same ones every year:

1.) Lose weight
2.) Exercise more
3.) Be more patient (and kind, and loving, and gentle and other assorted biblical directives)
4.) Cook more at home instead of eating out so much; and
5.) Contribute to World Peace

(I always throw the World Peace goal in there so I don't sound so completely self-centered. After all, I *am* trying to live more biblically).

What I have realized several months later is that I have made about as much progress on the first four resolutions as I have on the whole World Peace thing. The 15 pounds I should be losing is still hanging around, enjoying a leisurely lifestyle around my middle and clamoring for another bag of Doritos. On January 2, when I decided it was time to start exercising, I moved the treadmill in front of the TV in the basement, turned on a favorite sitcom for motivation--and sat on the couch to watch it. And for resolutions number three and four--well, all I can say is when I was in the fast food drive-thru lane yesterday I only honked my horn once at the slow driver in front of me. I guess that's *something*.

So what seems to be the issue with my resolutions? Why can't I make them stick? Perhaps, as the experts in the women's magazines tell me, I need to be more detailed and specific with my goals. I should devise objectives that are practical and reasonable and will not make me feel like an inadequate loser who is lucky to be able to function in society. So I took their advice and sat down recently to pen a more meticulous list of resolutions that I thought I would have a slight chance of actually accomplishing:

My NEW New Year's Resolutions
1.) Graciously accept all offers of dark chocolate, even though I really prefer milk chocolate
2.) Learn to say "arthroscopic shoulder surgery" without messing up
3.) Don't make ANY trips to the Social Security office or the Driver's License Bureau
4.) Be prepared to shout, "Don McLean!" whenever someone asks who sings "American Pie"
5.) Stop worrying about whether I should dust first, *then* vacuum, or vacuum first, *then* dust; and
6.) Contribute to World Peace (my conscience simply won't allow me to delete this one).

The NEW New Year's Resolutions also come with a new set of rules, like if I accomplish one, I can take a break for a month or so to gather my energies for the next one. And if I don't accomplish all six by December 31, I can carry them over with no penalties into next year.

With this system, World Peace may just have a chance.

LIFE IN GENERAL:
Making Waves

THE HOME IMPROVEMENT COMPATIBILITY TEST

Here's a startling but true fact for you: Men and women are *different*. And sometimes, this can cause conflict!

I know this because I, a woman, have spent over 20 years being married to a man. We discovered our fundamental differences soon after we were married by undertaking various home improvement projects together. If you really want to find out if your marriage will survive, skip the sessions with highly-paid professionals. You and your potential partner should just grab some tools and spend two days tearing off old musty wallpaper in a half bathroom only slightly larger than a box of Velveeta Cheese, like my husband and I did as newlyweds. If you still like each other after 48 hours, and no one flung wallpaper paste at anyone else in the process, you're good to go.

The problem boils down to this: What one person in the marriage (namely the man) thinks is a simple and straightforward job usually requires much more discussion, analysis and general mulling over (according to the woman). For example, THIS is how my husband believes one should go about painting a kitchen (our most recent project):

1. Pick out paint
2. Buy Paint
3. Move stuff out of the kitchen
4. Paint
5. Move stuff back into the kitchen
6. Break out the cookies and milk and turn on *The Golf Channel*.

Ideally, all six of these steps should take place over the course of one day, so there will still be time left in the weekend to go golfing.

On the other hand (WAY on the other hand, possibly on the other FOOT), I, as the female in the partnership, decided the following very different steps had to be taken in order to accomplish the same task:

1. Watch hours and hours of home and garden television shows that depict everyone in the United States and half of Canada avidly re-painting, re-modeling and generally re-everything-ing their homes.

2. Become inspired and announce in an urgent tone of voice that it is necessary to re-paint the unacceptable eggshell-colored kitchen walls as soon as possible, despite anxious look on husband's face.

3. Ask girlfriends (who have also been watching hours and hours of home and garden shows) what colors they think are "in."

4. Tour girlfriends' homes to review their recent paint choices and do a lot of nodding and saying things like, "Oh, that gold hue REALLY warms up this room!" and "That ragging effect is STUNNING!" and other things you only say after watching hours and hours of home and garden shows.

5. Traipse to the paint store to spend two and a half hours perusing the millions of paint samples and then close eyes and randomly select three to take home for consideration.

6. Go home and tape the sample swatches to the kitchen wall and curse the fact that the swatches are the size of a postage stamp and

I'm expected to radically change the room based on this microscopic bit of information. Let the swatches dangle on the wall for several days out of pure spite.

7. Ask husband what color he likes. "Brown."
8. Call girlfriends and ask what color they like. "Macadamia."
9. Traipse back to the paint store and request a sample quart of paint in color girlfriends like.
10. Paint a four foot section of one wall with sample paint. Step back and gasp in horror.
11. Repeat steps 9 and 10. Three more times.
12. Stare at kitchen walls, which have turned into a psychedelic checkerboard of "Camelback," "Soba," and "Onionskin" colors, and consider doing something I'll regret with masking tape.
13. Buy masking tape.
14. Go back to paint store and *beg* nice lady to please just choose paint *for* me. "Mackintosh."
15. Buy many paint brushes so I don't have to actually clean any brushes during the painting process; and then buy some of those irresistibly cute pink and fuzzy miniature roller brush thingys.
16. Engage husband in the task of moving the stove and refrigerator out of the kitchen, which he must do without rolling his eyes in response to the purchase of cute fuzzy roller brush thingys.
17. Go to bed because it's 2:00 a.m. and I just now finished cleaning the gunk that was behind the stove and the refrigerator.
18. Move rest of stuff out of kitchen. Get into serious squabbles with husband over number of useless items on kitchen counters (like the

canister set, which is purely decorative), who has to vacuum the two-inch layer of dust on top of the cabinets, and why husband's opinion on color was even requested, if "Brown" was going to be summarily rejected anyway.

19. Threaten to use masking tape.
20. Hire painter.

As you see, once again we were able to calmly recognize our areas of conflict, come to a mature compromise (see step #20) and our marriage was saved, along with several rolls of masking tape. It may have taken three weeks of preparation, one actual day of painting and a month to put things back in place, but we are now the proud owners of a stunning, warmed-up kitchen and, *as a fabulous bonus*, we have added to our wealth of knowledge on gender differences.

Anyone need some cute pink and fuzzy roller brush thingys?

SOME THINGS JUST CAN'T BE CONTAINED

I have a home full of homeless objects.

Today, as I made a clean sweep through the house, I made note of the following items that had not been returned to an appropriate residence of their own:

- a tape measure
- somebody's orthodontic retainer
- eight pens and pencils
- five old magazines
- a pair of sunglasses
- a half-eaten bag of cookies
- an extension cord
- a bottle of nail polish
- a box of thank you notes
- a dog brush
- an ink jet printer cartridge and
- a bowl of batteries (don't ask).

Items like these just run amok in my house. They've been recently used, or someone has the intention of using them soon, so they float in object limbo. They clutter the counters, the end tables and the desks, free and unfettered, refusing to be put away. My homeless objects and I have been in a constant battle for domination, and I have been on the losing end.

But things are going to change: I have recently been energized, enlightened and empowered and *I am about to impose martial law on all homeless objects under my roof.*

This new aspiration started a few weeks ago, when I found myself among a group of women sitting in a living room, watching an organization guru demonstrate various household containers that are public enemy #1 to homeless objects. As I flipped through the container catalog the guru handed out, I began to dream of all my homeless objects being neatly and fashionably stored away. I was lured by the thought of cookies that could be first placed in a beautiful cookie jar and then actually remain there for a time before being devoured unmercifully by my teenage son. I began to think it possible that the scattered items on my bathroom vanity could be controlled if only they had their own heavy-duty storage bin. I felt my heart pounding faster when I realized if I purchased the handy caddy for the middle of my dining room table, I would always know the whereabouts of the salt and pepper shakers. And when the guru presented the supersized six-slot desk organizer as the pièce de resistance, I broke out in a cold sweat and found myself begging to take it home as a cash and carry item. In fact, at the end of the demonstration I practically knocked the other women down, checkbook in hand, ready to fork over great wads of cash for the promise of a home where remote controls are corralled, magazines and newspapers are always sorted, and hats and gloves are kept in check.

These containers are the solution I've been waiting for. So what if it costs me my entire paycheck? I know as soon as my organizers arrive, I can enforce military rule on all homeless objects so they will march in an orderly manner to their new quarters, and only come out when ordered to do so.

My husband thinks I'm being overly optimistic and that I'm wasting money on my new system. He has hinted strongly that the problem lies not with the *objects* in our house, but with the habits of the *people* who reside in our house.

Well.

I wonder if they make a container for wet blankets...

PILLOW FIGHT

Acquiring a new mattress and a few pillows used to be an easy, low-tech process.

When I was about to go away to college, for instance, I bought a single-bed-shaped foam cushion that was rumored to have a few springs of some kind inside it. I picked it up at a garage sale for about $10, and it served me well for four years. I believe I had to burn it after graduation, but that's not important. The point is, it was a straightforward transaction. I swiped a pillow from my bed at home and I was all set. When we got married, my husband and I simply used the mattress and pillows that he had bought with his queen-sized bed several years before, and then in the early 1990s we just followed the pack and did what almost everyone else did: we bought a waterbed mattress. When we reached the point that we needed a crane every morning to hoist ourselves out of the v-shaped groove in the middle of the bed and the pillows we were using had lost their will to live, we knew it was time to go shopping.

One step into a mattress store and it became immediately apparent that I had not kept up with the many advances in "Sleep Technology." I didn't know my sleep number. Or the difference between independent spring coiling and pocket coiling. I didn't remember what memory foam was. I stared blankly at a TV while some talking sheep tried to teach me about the importance of "body contouring" and "edge support." And then there was the dizzying array of reversible pillow-top options. Clearly, I had been asleep at the wheel when I should have been paying attention to such high-tech developments in the mattress industry. All I can say is thank goodness for those persistent Swedish Scientists. They're the ones who, perhaps because they enjoy more hours of darkness in their climate, dedicated their entire *careers* to mattress research and development for the sole purpose of giving me another reason to hit the snooze alarm in the morning.

Once we carefully compared all the features and benefits of each mattress and chose one to fit our lifestyle and body mass index needs perfectly (OK, we chose the one that LOOKED the most comfortable), we were ready to pick out pillows. Times have changed in the pillow industry as well. The first lesson in modern pillow shopping is that if there is more than one adjective used to describe the pillow, the price is allowed to triple, or correspond directly with the number of adjectives, whichever is greater. For example, a standard "down pillow" will cost you approximately $9.95, while a "Sleep Zone Ultra Select Organic Gel-Coated Microfiber Pillow" will cost you approximately one month's salary. The second lesson is that you are now required to take and pass the manufacturer's special online "Pillow Profile" assessment before the appropriate pillow can be released into your custody with completed adoption papers. Thanks to our Pillow Profile, now everyone in cyberspace knows I have allergies and a freak-of-nature neck problem, and that dear hubby is battling a slight tendency to snore (and I am being *extremely* kind with that description).

When we finally brought our state-of-the-art purchases home and set them up, we discovered the old sheets didn't fit the thicker mattress and the old pillowcases weren't big enough to hold all that organic microfiber.

I'm told I'll have to go buy some 100% Egyptian Combed Cotton Extra Deep 400 Thread Count Hypoallergenic Fitted Sheets with Satin Piping and Coordinating Ultra King PillowSurrounds.

It's enough to make a person lose sleep.

SECOND SHOWER

I've been thinking about getting remarried.

This could come as a slight shock to my husband of almost 20 years. He's been a wonderful partner, don't get me wrong. But I've attended several wedding showers in the past few months and let me tell you-- sometimes even the best of spouses can't compare to a complete set of new high end cookware or a color-coordinated ensemble of fluffy, super-size bath towels.

Sure, my bridesmaids threw a terrific wedding shower for me long ago (Note to Jackie and Rita--I still owe you for requiring me to make a cake from scratch in front of everyone in attendance--an exercise in futility if there ever was one). I appreciated all those gifts, although I recall receiving one kitchen item, which someone later explained was a "grease separator," that I had absolutely no idea how to use. Still don't.

But as I watched the recent bride-to-be unwrap gift after fabulous gift, I found myself tempted to put down my glass of punch, stealthily crawl under the tables and abscond with the 600-thread count sheet set she just received. I repressed thoughts of donning a black ski mask and swiping her new microwave oven under cover of darkness. And I had to restrain myself from yelling "Mouse!" so all the women at the shower would flee, leaving me alone to scarf up the high-speed smoothie maker, pewter candlesticks and plush his-and-her bathrobes like a hungry teenage boy at an all-you-can-eat buffet.

It's just that, after being married this long, my crock pot is caput, the towels have given up their will to live and the non-stick pans are sticking. I don't need the new husband; I just need the cool new stuff! It gets me thinking about an innovative concept that could really catch on: Wives who have been married for more than 15 years or so could get their bridesmaids back together and throw a Second Shower. A Second Shower would allow us not-so-newlyweds to replenish our household items with newer models, without the hassle of trading in our well-trained and broken-in hubbies for uh, well, newer models.

At a Second Shower, everyone would bring a household gift for exchange. There would be different rules to follow for this type of shower, such as:

1. No mystery kitchen utensils allowed. Anyone bringing an unrecognizable kitchen tool (at least to MY Second Shower) will be punished by having to separate grease.
2. Nothing advertised on late night TV qualifies as a Second Shower gift. Ever.
3. If you don't need or can't use any one item, you can trade with someone else. I myself would be more than willing to exchange any steam iron I receive for practically anything else you get.
4. No post-shower thank you notes are required.
5. Cake *is* required. And so is ice cream. Lots of it.

I think the idea of a Second Shower like this would be extremely popular. And the biggest advantage of the Second Shower would be that you don't have to actually have a Second Wedding. So relax, honey. And rest assured--I have zero desire for a Second *Baby* Shower.

BAD HAIR

I came across an old baby photo of mine the other day that made me gaze in disbelief. There I was, with a full head of shiny, bouncy, beautiful curls, reminiscent of Shirley Temple. What happened, I wondered, to all that pretty hair I once had?? I suspect it was a one-time photo-op collaboration involving my mom, 25 sponge rollers and a full jar of Dippity-Do, because I now possess stick-straight dirty dishwater brown hair bearing no resemblance to that photo. I have Bad Hair. Not the kind that comes and goes, as in Bad Hair DAYS. No. That would be manageable. I have the full-time Chronic Bad Hair, the kind that never leaves and never even *considers* a vacation.

Bad Hair does not respond to traditional coaxing and prodding. You have to get mean with it. You have to buy at least a wagon full of different kinds of shampoos, conditioners gels and other treatments to beat it into submission. I have so many such bottles overcrowding the shower that I sometimes have to take a few out just so I can get in.

Bad Hair also needs a special kind of consistent haircut that makes it stay in line. For years, I have been wandering from stylist to stylist, hoping to find someone who could successfully deal with my duck tail neckline, tame my cowlicks, thin out the unexplainable wads of hair that develop over my ears, remember that I like my bangs fringe-y and not blunt, give me an overall cut that is low maintenance and give me a perm that is not too tight but will last for six months. I ask you, is this unreasonable? I can tell by the blank stares I get from some of these stylists that they think I am probably someone who needs to seek some counseling. Soon.

But I bravely go on, making appointment after appointment with renewed hope that This Time Things Will Be Different: I will get that elusive style that I can actually duplicate the next day. The new products I am talked into will actually work according to the hyped-up description on the bottles. And my husband will actually notice I got a jazzy new haircut, instead of raising an eyebrow and asking if I feel okay. The latest stylist does show some promise. She has scored some points by agreeing with me that yes, so far there are not many gray hairs on my head. She and I have even talked about a new hair color to replace the dirty dishwater hue.

A girl can dream, can't she?

BABY BOOM

As I was waiting in the endless grocery store checkout line the other day, casually reading the tabloid headlines and trying to ignore the choir of chocolate candy bars calling my name, I noticed an entire magazine cover devoted to celebrities who are "Moms After 40!" There they were, in their immaculate designer clothes and professionally applied make-up, smiling broadly with new babies in their arms and proclaiming all the glorious advantages of having an infant when you're well into your 40s, or even 50s.

I think the lives of these women must be radically different than mine. I am a woman pushing 50, and I know I could not survive another round of infanthood.

When I was in my 20s, I temporarily lost my mind and decided to have two babies in less than two years so my memories of their first months are a blurry collage of sleepless nights, emergency room visits, episodes of colic, and arguments with my husband about whose turn it was to get up in the middle of the night. Thank goodness we captured much of that time period on videotape or I would have no recollection of say, 1991 to 1994. I believe I was perpetually clothed in a baby-formula-stained robe and could take a shower only on the rare occasions when both babies were asleep and I wasn't. My house was a wreck, and some days I could barely string an intelligent sentence together. No one would have dreamed of putting me on a magazine cover unless it was "Lifestyles of the Tired and Disheveled." I survived, but only because I had 20-something stamina.

Now that I'm older, I know that a baby would take much more energy than I can muster and would completely disrupt my 40-something routine. I enjoy going to bed by 11:00 p.m. and actually sleeping in that bed for at least six consecutive hours. I like making a decision to go somewhere, and five minutes later, I can just go. If I don't cook, nobody goes hungry or cries (hardly ever, anyway). And I am rarely seen with spit-up on my shirt collars these days.

I was reminded of my lack of baby stamina just last weekend when my unencumbered lifestyle came to a complete halt while I cared for my seven-month-old niece Julia. She's as cute as a bug and has a sunny personality that can light up a room, but I am not afraid to admit that by the time I handed her back to her mother 27 hours later, I was whipped. Julia was still full of get-up-and-go, and I was the cranky one who needed a nap.

I wish those aging celebrity women all the luck in the world. But I'm guessing that even with an army of nannies, maids and cooks to help them, some of those ladies are still destined to end up sleep-deprived, un-showered and living in PJs.

Now THAT would be a magazine cover I could relate to.

EXTREME MEDICINE CABINET MAKEOVER

I saw a segment on the news the other day that really hit home. The report highlighted a 55-year-old man who continues to participate in all kinds of intense physical activities, despite multiple sports injuries and surgeries. The man's doctor could only shake his head and declare his patient had something called "Boomer-itis"--a newly-coined term meaning, in my rough translation, "middle-aged person in denial, resulting in great bodily harm and massive medical bills."

My husband and I are displaying symptoms of that very condition. Last weekend, for example, we played golf, worked in the yard, rode bikes and moved in some new furniture. But then on Sunday night, faced with rotator cuffs that were no longer rotating and arthritic knees that refused to bend, we discovered our heating pads were missing in action, we had no aspirin in the house AND the only thing we had for our blisters was an old box of Garfield band aids. We nearly came to blows over who would get the one ice pack we own and who would have to use a bag of frozen peas.

There are other clues that we are heading down the Boomer-itis path. Our trips to the chiropractor have become more frequent. We have caught ourselves at dinner parties extolling the virtues of the new nighttime combination pain reliever/sleep aids, and discussing various other conditions that end in "–itis." Our vocabulary now contains such intriguing words as "Chondroitin" and "Glucosamine." Yet our medicine cabinet is still filled with children's medical remedies, even though the kids are well beyond the boo-boo years of skinned knees, earaches and pink eye. We are clearly and pathetically unprepared for this phase of our lives.

It's time to break through our denial. Just like ABC's Ty Pennington does in the *Extreme Home Makeover* show every Sunday night, we must radically change our surroundings and adapt to our current situation. In order to take on Boomer-itis, we'll need to conduct an Extreme Medicine Cabinet Makeover.

I can picture it now. Ty will send my husband and me on a two-day trip to a rehabilitation hospital while he works his magic. Upon returning home, our faces will register utter shock and surprise as Ty flings open the door of the new 8'x10' Boomer-ready medicine pantry and reveals...two dozen boxes of ace bandages and a carton of Ben-Gay! Where once there was an emergency bottle of Ipecac and some Pedialyte, there'll be cases of eight-hour heat patches and gallon jugs of Ibuprofen. No more insect bite sprays and baby aspirin--they've been replaced with foot spas and mini-saunas. And in the freezer: TWO cold packs with detachable Velcro straps and suede lining!

We'll get all teary-eyed and express overwhelming gratitude for our new his-and-her heated recliners that also give full body massages. And, oh my gosh, when Ty leads us to the garage--we'll discover a lifetime supply of extra-strength multi-vitamins that are perfectly suited to our ages, genders and joint conditions! What a great public health service Ty will be providing for us Boomers-In-Denial. My husband and I will be jumping for joy. Only not too much or we'll have to break out the frozen peas.

SKIN DEEP

I went shopping in a big city recently. Now, I usually spend most of my big city shopping time in the super-sized bookstores, when I am not following behind my daughter as she attempts to persuade me why I absolutely HAVE TO buy her those purple Bermuda shorts that all the girls are wearing, even though it's 30 degrees outside. But on this particular outing, I happened onto a new store in a hoity-toity mall that took me so by surprise I just had to venture in.

It was a 5,000 square foot store dedicated solely to skin care products.

There were thousands of products for women, hundreds for men, and probably several dozen for my cat. There were oils and creams and toners and gels, potions for dry skin, oily skin and presumably just-right skin, and FDA watch-list herbal concoctions for every condition. Shelves were filled with products that would peel away, melt away or otherwise disintegrate any and all layers of your face and hands. On purpose. There was something for everyone. Got wrinkles and fine lines? No problem. These 400 products will take care of that.   Age spots or blemishes? Aisle Three. People were swarming in every nook and cranny, scooping up bottles and jars like sugared-up kids on Trick or Treat night. And in the back, happy women (and one slightly uncomfortable-looking man) were seated in reclining chairs with mud masks on their faces, while attendants in white lab coats bustled around them.

As I stood there wondering how that man explains to his football buddies that he pays money for someone to apply mud to his face, one of those bustling attendants sidled up to me. She must have seen me coming a mile away. She had astutely profiled me as the slapdash, laissez-faire type of skin caretaker I am, and could somehow tell that I don't cleanse, tone and buff on a daily basis or treat my under-eye circles and crow's feet as Public Enemies Number One and Two.

I was about to turn and run when she smiled an ultra-white smile and asked, in her twenty-something voice, "Ma'am, would you like to see some of the new products that can take years off your face?"

Blink, blink, blink went my eyes at the Bustler while I attempted to process that statement. Wow, I thought, I didn't even merit a "Miss"--I'm a full-fledged Ma'am now. And not just any old Ma'am--I'm a Ma'am who obviously has too many years piled up on her face and shouldn't waste another minute looking so hideous!

It was a defining moment. I stared as the Bustler held out a magic skin-altering formula for me to trial. And then…

Thirty minutes later I left that store with two bags full of Super Skin Tonics guaranteed to make me look 25 again before sundown. It's an immense relief knowing that I will soon be mistaken for my daughter's sister.

Now all I need is some purple Bermuda shorts.

LEFT BEHIND

I've been left behind.

At one time, I kept fairly good pace with technology. Dealing with computers, fax machines and cell phones did not make me break into hives. I could run all the appliances in my house without ending up in a fetal position. I could even program my own VCR without assistance from my children. But now it seems technology is racing ahead of me at lightning speed. I can no longer keep up with my upgrades or down with my downloads. I can't figure out how to choose my own cell phone ring, a computer error message has the power to paralyze me, and I can't even take a picture with my own camera without consulting a 30-page manual.

I'm thinking it's time to give up, wave the white flag, and come out with my hands up. I should have predicted this ultimate surrender to the technology gods based on my initial entrance into the world of computers. It was way back in high school, when I was simply trying to make a smiling face out of hundreds of letter X's using a prehistoric Radio Shack TRS-80 computer that had a cassette recorder for memory storage. When I was just about to push the button that would make the X's curve into a triumphant grin on the screen, the cassette ribbon unraveled and the recorder promptly ate nine weeks of work.

Now, while the gadgets and gizmos in my house continue to reproduce and morph from one version to the next faster than I can devour a plate of chocolate chip cookies, I am sitting on the sidelines watching the techno-parade go by. Even my television remote controls have moved on without me. One night last week I wandered out to the living room to watch a boring TV show that would hopefully lull my stubborn brain to sleep. But I couldn't watch the boring TV show, because I DIDN'T KNOW HOW TO TURN ON THE TV! Let me just pause here while that sinks in.

I really couldn't turn on my own television set.

The one previous remote control had multiplied into five, and they were splayed all over the coffee table, mocking me. I punched several thousand buttons on each remote, to no avail. All I got was a glowing blue screen with no sound. I couldn't even do it the old-fashioned way by actually getting up off the couch and pressing the ON button. It was 2:00 a.m., and I was desperate so I did what all good wives would do: I stomped into the bedroom, woke up my husband and made him turn on the set for me.

The morning after the TV incident, I sought solace in my comparatively low-tech vehicle. After all, I had mastered its power locks and windows long ago. But then I accidentally pressed the emergency *OnStar* button when I meant to open the garage door. The nice lady on the line understood my situation, gave me a refresher course on the buttons and forgave me for my modern technology learning disability.

Hey…I wonder if she could help me turn on my TV?

EXERCISE IN FUTILITY

I believe in exercise.

Unfortunately, my body doesn't.

This disagreement between my brain and the rest of my body parts has been brewing ever since I turned 40 a few years back. Up until that point, my brain and my body had this nifty little arrangement whereby my brain would decide to do something physical and my body would happily comply without complaint. For years I could snag throws at first base, feel the "burn" with Jane Fonda and run endless boring miles on a treadmill with nary a peep from my muscles and joints. Nowadays, when my brain says, "Just Do It," my hips, knees and shoulders say, "Over my dead body," and then proceed to take me closer to that end. Every time I try a new form of good-for-me exercise, my body revolts and throws roadblock after roadblock in my way, until I am at the point where I could give up and become a full-blown couch potato whose only exercise comes from pressing buttons on the remote control while shaking the last crumbs from the Doritos bag into my slothful mouth.

For instance, at one time Pilates held the esteemed honor of being my favorite (or more aptly, my least-disliked) exercise. It toned my muscles, gave me energy and bonus! I could take a power nap for the last five minutes of cool-down. Now, I can't attend the class without taking more-than-the-approved-number of Ibuprofen beforehand, wearing a compression band on my left elbow and using a wimpy rubber ball instead of the recommended five-pound weight for arm exercises or else my right rotator cuff will stage a protest and stop rotating altogether. Jogging is out of the question, as my knees have devised a way to inflate what feels like Jello balloons under my kneecaps after about five minutes, making me run a lot like Murphy, our neighbor dog who has been hit on the road something like five times and now hobbles on three legs. And don't ask why I can no longer even attempt the "Cobra," the "Table Top," or the "Cow-Cat" positions in Yoga Class.

I try to sweet talk my body into submission by plying it with daily doses of Super Maximum Glucosamine and Chondroitin, getting full-body massages and promising it a dip in the hot tub at the end of the proposed activity. I have put gel pads in the heels of my tennis shoes and tamed my jogging down to mere walking but my hips still creak.

My girlfriends in their 50s and 60s are no encouragement. They have given up on challenging exercise and now count grocery shopping on their lunch hours as the most strenuous activity they attempt on a regular basis. They are convinced that we should not fight our aging bodies' natural aversion to exercise, and we should instead slide into retirement holding a double glazed donut in one hand and a plate of fettuccine alfredo in the other.

I'll bet my rotator cuff would have no problem with that.

SENDING A GREETING CARD IN 20 MINUTES OR LESS

To my brother-in-law Stan--Happy Birthday. You won't be getting a card from me.

It's not that I don't like you. You make the best smoked turkey on the planet. What's not to like?? It's just that I have some kind of genetic defect that prevents me from purchasing a greeting card, adding a clever little note, signing my name and popping it into the mail before another 12 months has elapsed. I've done everything I can to streamline the process and make it foolproof. I try to keep a stock of cards on hand. I faithfully write the dates on my calendar. But inevitably, I miss the deadlines and I am stuck holding a get well card for someone who is back to running marathons, a baby card for a child entering Kindergarten, and a wedding card for a couple celebrating their 3rd anniversary. I just can't seem to stay focused on the process.

I truly had the best of intentions this time. I had laid out a condensed plan that involved four easy steps and a 20-minute time frame:
1.) Select a card from the card box at home
2.) Sign, seal, stamp and address the card
3.) Put the card in the mailbox
4.) Go reward myself with a dozen monster cookies from the bakery.

It should have worked, especially since there was the promise of cookies at the finish line. I started a week before the B-day. On Day One, I went to select the card and realized I didn't have an appropriate not-too-serious-but-not-too-sarcastic-card-for-a-50-something-man in stock.

Cut to Day Two, when I found myself perusing the endless choices in a greeting card store. There were cards for absolutely every occasion--cards that made me feel even more guilty for my apparent lack of concern for my fellow man. I didn't realize there was a card I should have sent to my neighbors when their mailbox was hit by a snow plow. How rude that I never sent the card meant to help my brother cope with his dog's outbreak of fleas. And I was feeling just plain cold-hearted about not sending the special card to my two-year-old niece when she accomplished potty-training. I left the store with 27 greeting cards and a burdened soul.

On Day Three, I couldn't remember where I had put the bag with all the cards in it.

On Days Four and Five, I found the bag in the back seat of the car. It took hours to find a pen that worked and hours more to find the correct address. Then I discovered all I had were outdated 37-cent stamps, so I asked my husband to purchase a roll of new stamps. Meanwhile, I abandoned the card on the no-man's-land area of the kitchen counter and went to watch *American Idol*.

By the time Day Seven rolled around and my husband brought the stamps home, I couldn't recall why I needed them so urgently.

But those monster cookies were great.

WHAT'S HIS IS MINE

I believe that a successful marriage must include openness, honesty, and mutual sharing of belongings. In order for a union to last, there should be absolutely no secrets between the partners, and household possessions should not be segregated. I think my husband of 20-plus years would agree.

Then why won't he tell me where his Sharpie Marker is??

I know he has one somewhere, but he insists on hiding it like a national treasure that needs multiple impenetrable layers of security protecting it from a family of would-be thieves. To access it, you must give three days advance notice, provide two forms of identification and produce a written contract guaranteeing its safe return.

I don't get it. We've only lost his marker a few times. Once, the kids took it to school to color in the former Soviet Union on their map of the world, and it understandably ended up dried out and useless after that experience. And perhaps once last summer I took it outside to mark labels on seedling pots and maybe it got left out in the rain. Maybe even twice. But is that any reason to move the Sharpie from hiding place to hiding place, like it's a member of the government's witness protection program?

That's not the only thing he hides from me. There's the stash of sugar cookies in the console of his truck. There's my favorite cinnamon gum in the linen closet. And he thinks I don't know this, but that high end silver grill lighter that he won as a door prize but is really better suited to light my scented candles in the kitchen--resides in his bottom desk drawer under some old golf score cards.

Why all the secrecy? I don't understand it. We are in a committed relationship that relies on integrity of character. His overwhelming need to conceal these personal possessions is just mystifying.

What? Oh, sure, I hide a few things too. But *my* objects are critical to the success of the household and must be protected at all costs. Scissors, tape and working pens are habitually on the Missing Persons list and therefore justifiably live a cloak and dagger life on top of the utility cabinet. My fingernail clippers are restricted to a radius of three feet from my vanity or a series of alarm bells will sound and the local law enforcement will be automatically notified. Of course it's a necessity to keep emergency shopping cash in an envelope in with the cleaning supplies (a VERY secure spot). And the bag of bite-size Snickers bars in the coffee cup in the curio cabinet? Well, every woman understands the fundamental value of chocolate in a crisis, real or otherwise, and no smart man would ever question that theory.

Does this veil of secrecy between us point to marital distress? Are we on shaky ground, headed for the marriage scrap heap?

Nah. I'll just have a mini-Snickers, grab some shopping money and everything will be OK.

And maybe I'll pick up a Sharpie while I'm out.

AS SEEN ON TV

I need to start sleeping or I'm going to go broke.

Let me explain. I recently experienced a week-long bout of insomnia. No matter what I tried, I would end up wide awake at 2:30 in the morning, twiddling my thumbs and humming old show tunes. I counted sheep. I tried reading the scintillating financial reports that come with my quarterly investment fund statements. I even played a tape of Neil Diamond's Greatest Hits to no avail. Nothing sent me off to dreamland. So, after consultation with my loving and considerate husband that ended with one of us saying, in a rather terse manner I might add, "If you're going to insist on humming "The Sound of Music," can you do it from the couch in the living room?!?" I moved to the couch in the living room. And then I turned on the television.

Little did I know the opportunities I had been missing by choosing to sleep. Over the course of seven nights, I discovered I was blithely unaware of some serious problems in my life! For instance, on the first night I was dismayed to learn that I am an ignoramus in the personal care department. I have unknowingly been filing my nails with a standard issue nail file when I should be filing them with an egg-shaped automatic filer that fits *neatly into the palm of my hand!* Of course I did not want to risk the public humiliation of bad nails, so for $29.95 I snapped up two egg filers and forever eliminated the danger of accidentally maiming those sensitive cuticle areas. And, with the purchase of the tweezers with the built-in spotlight, I can now tweeze my eyebrows at 3:00 a.m. while surfing the TV channels for additional items to improve my life.

I was hooked, and it was only sleepless night number one.

The next few nights had a laundry theme. I HAD to spend $19.95 on a shaving watchamacallit for my embarrassing shedding sweaters, a measly $12.95 (because I *acted now*) for six balls of lint-collecting static-ending gizmos for the dryer, and $49.99 for a lifetime supply of stain treater that will put an end to all my stubborn laundry challenges forever. *Or my money back!!*

And, if it weren't for my sleeplessness on nights four and five, I would have never considered there was a better way to keep my fresh vegetables fresh. Turns out there is, and for the low price of $39.95 I bought some space-age plastic bags and will never have to deal with brown bananas again! By night seven, I was not only awake, I was spinning salads, slicing onions with a samurai sword and mixing questionable drink concoctions in a revolutionary, yet surprisingly user-friendly mini-blender.

Although I have run up quite the credit card bill, at least I'm feeling productive while I'm not sleeping. Sooner or later, though, this middle-of-the-night commotion will awaken my slumbering husband.

Good thing all he'll have to do is clap his hands to turn on the lights...

THE GIFT BUYING GENE
Semi-confidential Memo to My Husband:

Darling,

After being married to you for more than two decades, I have come to understand that you as a man have different genetics than I do as a woman. You, for example, are the proud owner of genes that enable you to a.) Burp loudly; b.) Change a flat tire in a downpour; and c.) Remember every stroke of every score of every hole you've ever golfed. I, as a female, possess the genes that allow me to a.) Simultaneously make supper, help a child with Algebra and dash off a note to my congressman; b.) Ask for directions; and c.) Involuntarily roll my eyes at the mention of every stroke of every score of every hole you've ever golfed.

I also have the Gift Buying Gene that allows me to thoughtfully select the appropriate present for anyone from a newborn to a newlywed couple to a retiree. You do not possess that gene. Instead, you have the instinct to ignore events that require gift-giving, and hope with all your being that the events will pass by with no one noticing that you did nothing. This evasion tactic works just fine, and I am happy to assume the household gift-buying duties, *as long as I am not the recipient of the gift*. Therefore, I am providing you with these helpful gift-buying tips that may increase your odds of receiving a smile rather than a frown from me on any future birthdays and/or holidays:

1.) Do not attempt to cover up your lack of interest in gift-buying by announcing "Birthdays are no big deal" or "This holiday is a blatant commercialized scam to get me to buy a $4.00 card" or "In some countries, it's considered bad luck to give gifts."

2.) Do not wait until the last minute. Let's recall one Mother's Day when you rushed out at 7:00 a.m. to purchase a card. You ended up standing in line at Kroger's with a dozen other sheepish men who had just picked through the remnant cards. I believe the card I received that year read, "To the Woman Who's Like a Mother To Me."

3.) Do not ignore any photos of jewelry that may get cut out of a catalog and taped to your bathroom mirror. This is a scientific attempt to overcome your gene deficiency through the use of precise environmental prompts.

4.) Gift cards are your friends. They can prevent such tragedies as the time when you bought some kind of plaid dress for me that looked like a castoff from *Little House on the Prairie*. Not to mention that it was four sizes too big.

5.) Gifts that are more suited for you do not count as actual gifts to me. In case you're still wondering, that automatically eliminates the new putter, lawn mower and cordless drill ideas.

I hope these tips are helpful, sweetheart. If not, you may unintentionally discover something else about my womanly design--the Pouting Gene.

PURSE EVOLUTION

I did something last week that I've never done before. I bought a purse.

That may not seem unusual to some of you, but to me it's wild and crazy because *I didn't even need one!*

Buying a purse for no good reason represents complete and utter transformation in my purse buying habits. I don't understand what happened. In fact, Darwin himself may have trouble explaining my evolution from a basic prehistoric "I Couldn't-Care-Less-About-My-Purse" person to a present-day obsessed "I-Gotta-Have-Another-One" person.

In the beginning, way back in what I call my Early Gimmegumazoic Era, my only interest in purses was my Grandma's pocketbook. It was plain brown leather and weighed about 29 pounds, but it had a secret middle section where she kept gum for the grandkids. However, most of the time my three older brothers beat me to the Chiclets and all I was left with was a nasty stick of Black Jack.

In the midst of my Tomboyazoic Era, I considered purses nothing but a necessary evil. The only purse I could tolerate was a denim purse I inherited from my older cousin Jenny. I kept a slingshot, a Rubik's cube and my Roller Rink pass in it. And if anybody made fun of it, or me, I was prone to slugging them.

The next real purse era I passed into was the frantic Mommazoic Era, when additional life forms began to flourish in my house. Survival of the fittest meant my purses had to be gigantic and double as diaper bags, toy boxes and book repositories for the kids. I could produce a pacifier, a hair ribbon and/or a John Deere toy tractor from my mega-purse at a moment's notice. But these purse/bags were purely functional, and they lived out a maximum six months of drudgery until they were replaced by the next unsuspecting purse/bag.

Based on this historic data, one could assume I had no genetic predisposition toward collecting purses. Yet I have clearly crossed over to the purse dark side, where I now find it necessary to have a purse for every occasion, and some for occasions I'll have to invent. I know all the brands, I scour the sale flyers for bargains and I was recently spotted battling other members of the female species for dominance at a designer purse clearance table deep in the heart of Chinatown.

So what caused this drastic (and slightly shameful) mutation in my DNA? Perhaps it's because I'm now smack dab in the middle of the Girlfrienda Influencazoic Era. It turns out this is the strongest, most powerful era of all, and resistance is futile. My association with six women in particular has succeeded in switching on my Purse Buying Gene and has directly contributed to the purse population explosion in my closet. These girlfriends taught me the ropes (or the straps) of purse selection and now there's no turning back.

Oh well. At least I'll have plenty of gum for all my grandkids. And their kids. And...

THINKING OUTSIDE THE BOX

Someone recently sent to me a video of a comedian who was comparing a man's brain to a woman's brain. A man's brain, the comedian said, consists of separate boxes that never, under any circumstances, touch each other. The boxes are neatly labeled Job, Family, Work, Play, etc. and when a man opens one, he deals only with that subject and has to close that box before he can move on to a different box. On the other hand, a woman's brain is always humming, he said, like a giant information superhighway. It's a ball of wire that is constantly firing and connecting everything to everything else and it never slows downs and it never even sleeps.

Hmmmm… this could be the reason why my husband and I have many conversations like this one that took place in the car a few weeks ago, after we had dinner with our teens and they went their separate ways:

ME: *(with brain cells buzzing)* You know honey, I have been thinking about how our lives are about to drastically change. Soon the kids will be in college and we'll hardly see them. It will be just the two of us. No running around after them, no activities to attend. Won't that be odd? I'm a little concerned. Were you thinking the same thing just now?

HUSBAND: *(deeply entrenched in his Driving Box)* No.

ME: *(with brain cells now rapidly picking up speed)* You mean you've *never* thought about our empty nest? It's right around the corner! We need to plan! We need to get organized! We should be thinking about a smaller home and doing something wild and crazy like buying an RV or a Harley!

HUSBAND: *(trying desperately not to jump from the Driving Box to the Dealing with a High Maintenance Wife Box)* Okaaayyyy. Uh, honey, I'm driving. Can we talk about this later?

Now that I think about it, it seems our opposing brain operating systems guarantee conversational conflict in almost all areas of our married life. For example, I have noticed when he watches TV he can *only watch TV*--he is locked inside the Television Box in his brain. He is not thrilled when I watch TV next to him, because I need to discuss plot lines, poke fun at cheesy dialogue and ask him what I missed when I was off doing laundry. And when we're golfing he's all hunkered down in the confines of his Golfing Box, intensely focused on his swing technique and his score. He has no interest in listening to me comment on the weather, the lovely landscaping, the gnats flying into my eyes or the fact that golf is a ridiculous sport.

If he could just break down the walls of those boxes in his brain and learn to recognize my need to constantly converse, we'd be much better off.

I suppose I could also slow the rapid fire pace of my chattiness...

But that's thinking too far outside the box.

PICK A DATE, ANY DATE

My five girlfriends and I are trying to get together for dinner.

This is a task that has taken approximately three weeks to coordinate, because first of all, we're busy people. Secondly, we're all in different stages of life, which complicates matters. But mostly, we have a lot of trouble staying focused on the goal. For the most recent attempt, we started with a simple question, zipped through email: "What date does everyone have available for dinner?"

Friend #1 mentioned that she could make a week from Tuesday, if she didn't have to take her teenage daughter dress shopping for some upcoming school dance. That prompted a flurry of responses from all of us who wanted to know who her daughter would be going to the dance with, what type of dress she was looking for, and whether the kids at her school engage in that very popular but very disturbing bumping and grinding dance style.

Friend #2 said she couldn't make Tuesday because she had a dentist appointment that afternoon and would still be recovering from the effects of Novocain and if she couldn't enjoy the triple chocolate meltdown dessert we were sure to get after dinner, life would not be worth living.

Friend #3 had heard there was going to be a snowstorm that Wednesday so we should probably not pick that day. That comment spurred a lengthy conversation about the merits of living in Ohio in the winter and which Southern state would most likely be our ultimate retirement destination. (North Carolina won, by the way. It's warmer than Ohio, but still has four seasons).

Friend #4 wanted to look at two Thursdays from now because she was going to be busy watching grandchildren. There's a new baby among her grandchildren, so we insisted on seeing the latest photos and then commenting how much the new little one looked exactly like the others. Then we discovered Friend #5 would be getting her nails done that Thursday evening, which meant we all needed to weigh in on the newest trends in nail polish colors. It was a helpful conversation, as I was completely unaware that Mexican Jumping Bean was more of a sunset orange than a burnt sienna.

Then I checked *my* calendar. It's a great old-fashioned paper calendar. I've successfully avoided the less reliable electronic version, even though I have a multi-function phone/email/calendar device that's named after a fruit (to lure me into thinking it's good for me). In my opinion, electronic calendars just don't provide the same level of ease that paper calendars do. Of course I brought this up to the group, who supported my theory by citing specific examples of electronic calendar fiascos of their own.

Ten days into the conversation, we switched to attempting a lunch date instead of a dinner date. And finally, after consulting the Famer's Almanac, reading tea leaves and pinky-swearing, we found a workable time slot.

Now all we need to do is decide *where* we're going to eat.

WAVING THE WHITE SHEET

I give up.

I have tried for at least 30 years to do it, and it's just NOT going to happen. I've watched demonstrations from Martha Stewart, studied articles in women's magazines and even searched the internet for instructions, yet I'm still a miserable failure at it.

I cannot fold a fitted sheet.

Each attempt is a frightening matchup between woman and elastic, and woman loses every time. No matter how hard I try, the sheet in question ends up in a lumpy wad that refuses to lie flat on the shelf. Martha would most certainly click her tongue and wave a disapproving finger at the disheveled sheets in my linen closet.

I realize this little dilemma of mine is not going to make or break the economy, determine the outcome of peace negotiations in the Middle East, or affect who becomes the next American Idol. But still, my lack of domestic dexterity bothers me. I graduated from college. Twice. Why can't I master a nondescript piece of cloth??

When I really think about it, there are many other examples of household tasks that get the best of me. My Personal Domestic Failures list is quite lengthy and includes things like:
- Mending socks. Or seams. Or threading a needle, for that matter.
- Recording movies or shows directly from the TV. Too many remotes, too few brain cells.

- Making lump-free mashed potatoes. Or lump-free gravy to pour on them.
- Cooking a pan of hash browns without turning them into unrecognizable mush.
- Baking a blueberry pie that my husband would actually deem edible.
- Neatly tying a bow on a gift.
- Timing my housework so that all rooms are clean at the same time for at least 20 minutes.
- Arranging a vase of flowers so they don't look like they've just been through a hail storm.
- Dusting furniture without flunking the white glove test.
- Doing a day's worth of laundry without a Kleenex exploding in the washer, an ink pen leaking on a white t-shirt, or a glob of gum cementing to the dryer drum.

My high school Home Economics teacher would not be surprised at this list. Though she tried valiantly to convert me from domestic dodo to domestic diva, she witnessed me sew a sleeve on a blouse backward, make a pair of left-handed gloves, and create a Waldorf Salad that the Health Department would have condemned. I think I was the only female who received a B in that class.

Clearly, I need to purge these types of domestic activities from my life and move on. I should accept my personal limitations and acknowledge the fact that my DNA is completely missing the Homemaker Genes that other women possess. Therefore, I am hereby waving the white sheet, so to speak, and will no longer try to master household tasks that I have no hope of mastering.

I'm sure in my case, Martha would have to say *it's a good thing.*

A SPECIAL TRIBUTE

**To my dad, who loved to tell stories and was always ready with a joke.
A portion of the proceeds from this book will be donated to the
American Heart Association
in his memory.**

Taken from a column published in June, 2005

THE GIFT OF A LIVING WILL

Beneath the recent public cacophony surrounding Terri Schiavo and her family's clash over her right to live or die, my family continued in private mourning for my father, feeling fortunate.

My Dad was a giving man. He was married for 51 years to the love of his life, raised five kids with strong values, and worked hard to provide for us. He gave his time generously to the small town where he lived, serving in public office and volunteering as a fireman for over 30 years. He drove a fuel route for two decades, making friends with kids and dogs by handing out Tootsie Rolls at every stop. And when someone couldn't pay him for fuel, which was often, he filled their fuel tanks anyway because it was the right thing to do. He taught me how to bait a hook, how to drive a tractor and how to throw a baseball like a boy. He was a nature lover who fed birds and a people lover who told fish stories with the best of them.

But when Dad was young and healthy and headed for the Korean War, he started his lifelong habit of smoking. That choice haunted him in his later years, as he waged a different war with the resulting vascular disease that clogged and blocked his circulatory system at every turn. His body endured so many surgeries that his grandkids thought the purple scars racing up and down his legs, arms and chest looked like misshapen, off-track zippers. His last surgery--a procedure meant to choke off an aneurysm that had ballooned behind his left knee--was just one month before he died. My brother, my mom and I accompanied him to the hospital for that umpteenth time, joking with him and trying to erase the look of weariness and worry in his eyes. He hated hospitals and hated being sick.

Thirty days later, graduated from a walker to a cane, he was back in his garage workshop, happily constructing bird houses and wind chimes for anyone and everyone. My mom called him in to get ready for church. And then, in the middle of that ordinary scene, a sudden, severe headache descended on him and plunged us into the surreal world of high-speed ambulance rides, chaotic emergency rooms, and somber, too-quiet Critical Care Units. The situation deteriorated rapidly. By the time all of Dad's far-flung children and grandchildren made it to his side, eight hours had elapsed and he was no longer able to respond to us. Only his chest moved, expanding and contracting with the rhythm of a ventilator. "A massive bleed," the internist on duty told us matter-of-factly as we stood staring at a computer screen. He pointed his stubby pencil at the enemy: a large ghost-gray blotch covering most of the MRI image of my Dad's brain. "Sorry," the doctor said. "There's nothing we can do." Two more specialists examined my Dad and agreed--there was no hope. We slowly started to realize we would have a momentous decision to make.

Those of us who have been unwillingly initiated into the End-Of-Life Decisions Club can tell you nothing is matter-of-fact at that point in time. Mountains of medical and scientific data are obscured by dark clouds of emotion. How do you make a decision to deliberately disconnect machines and watch your loved one leave this world, and you, behind?

My father had given us an additional tool, however. He had a Living Will, specifically stating his wishes against artificially extending his life. We clung to those papers and read them over and over in his hospital room that night, staining the document with our salty tears. Clearly, he wanted no excessive means used to keep him alive but not living. It was right there in black and white, punctuated with his familiar signature at the bottom of the page.

Still, we waited. We were raised Catholic, and were now gathered at a Catholic hospital. The ethical questions swirled around us. What was the right thing to do here? And when? What does the Church say about Living Wills? Is it selfish to ignore his wishes? What would happen when the machines were turned off? Could we bear to watch? Should we hold out for a miracle? The kind internist, also Catholic, guided us gently through the decision making process. He spoke of heaven, of freedom from pain, of God's will. He counseled us to have lengthy, open discussions with each other and told us we all needed to be in complete agreement, or we were not to leave the room.

The hours passed. We took turns holding Dad's hands, stroking his hair and reminding him how much we loved him. The older grandchildren, ranging in age from 5 to 18, slipped in and out of his room, their young faces registering everything from wonder to fear to utter sadness. Twice, they circled his bed and sang to him: first a funny family favorite--"Do Your Ears Hang Low?" and then a melancholy version of "You Are My Sunshine," a song my Dad had sung to each one of them as babies. It was a painfully sweet demonstration of love and legacy and it made the adults in the room crumble.

Finally, as the clock closed in on 2:00 a.m., we came to the gut-wrenching consensus to give our own gift and let this wonderful man go, just as he wished. We called for the doctor, sent the grandkids out of the room and held Dad's hands once again. My mom bravely talked to him through her steady stream of tears as the doctor and nurse dutifully went about their business behind her. One by one, the beeping machines were turned off. We prayed, no-- *begged*, Dad would not struggle. He didn't. At 2:25 a.m. on Sunday, February 20, 2005, his battle-scarred heart came to a standstill after 72 years, 4 months and 18 days of work. He was free to go.

Despite our extreme sorrow, we look back on our experience with a surprising sense of gratitude. We are grateful we were there with Dad to coach him into the next life, grateful for the empathetic doctor God sent to us, grateful Dad went peacefully. But most of all, we were grateful for the act of love that is a Living Will. Without it, we would have added the torture of uncertainty to our decision, and we would have had to wrestle with that doubt for the rest of our lives.

There was no media free-for-all leading up to my father's passing, no congressional debate, no judicial reviews. His name did not become a household word, his situation was not discussed at company water coolers. Yes, there was a decision to remove his life support machines, but it was wrapped in the comforting knowledge that it was exactly what he wanted. It was the last gift he gave us, and the last gift we gave him.

And, as we filed out of his hospital room that early morning, grief just beginning to overtake us, our decision was validated one last time. We heard the sound of a lullaby on the hospital's PA system overhead, signaling that a new soul had joined the human race, just as his had departed.

We smiled, and felt strangely blessed.

CONTACT MARY BETH

"Witty and Inspiring!"

Mary Beth Weisenburger offers a variety of fun, inspirational and thoughtful presentations that will leave audiences uplifted and delighted. No matter what the size or composition of the audience, Mary Beth has something for everyone. Her interactive presentations range between 15 and 60 minutes in length and are well-suited for keynote, after-dinner or energizing opportunities.

To contact Mary Beth about a speaking engagement or book requests, to share a funny story, or to just shoot the breeze, email: Marybeth@marybethw.com

To sign up for email notices and receive updates on Mary Beth's columns and future books, email: Mail@marybethw.com

To contact Mary Beth by good old-fashioned Snail Mail, write to:

Mary Beth Weisenburger
FreeBird Publishing and Promotions
22273 Road D
Continental OH 45831

Phone and fax: (419)596-4386